LINESTORM PLAYWRIGHTS PRESENT

GO PLAY OUTSIDE

T0346481

LINESTORM PLAYWRIGHTS PRESENT

GO PLAY OUTSIDE

TWENTY-FIVE SHORT PLAYS WRITTEN FOR THE GREAT OUTDOORS

**Edited and with an Introduction by
Lolly Ward**

APPLAUSE
THEATRE & CINEMA BOOKS
Guilford, Connecticut

Published by Applause Theatre & Cinema Books
An imprint of Globe Pequot, the trade division of
The Rowman & Littlefield Publishing Group, Inc.
4501 Forbes Blvd., Ste. 200
Lanham, MD 20706
www.rowman.com

Distributed by NATIONAL BOOK NETWORK

British Library Cataloguing in Publication Information available

Library of Congress Cataloging-in-Publication Data

Names: Ward, Lolly, editor.
Title: Go play outside : twenty-five short plays written for the great
  outdoors / edited and with an introduction by Lolly Ward.
Other titles: At head of title: Linestorm Playwrights present
Description: Guilford, Connecticut : Applause, [2022] | Series: Applause
  acting series
Identifiers: LCCN 2021038464 (print) | LCCN 2021038465 (ebook) | ISBN
  9781493061433 (paperback) | ISBN 9781493061440 (epub)
Subjects: LCSH: American drama—21st century. | One-act plays, American.
Classification: LCC PS627.O53 G6 2022 (print) | LCC PS627.O53 (ebook) |
  DDC 812/.04108—dc23
LC record available at https://lccn.loc.gov/2021038464
LC ebook record available at https://lccn.loc.gov/2021038465

∞™ The paper used in this publication meets the minimum requirements of
American National Standard for Information Sciences—Permanence of Paper
for Printed Library Materials, ANSI/NISO Z39.48-1992

Contents

Introduction

Four years ago, a short play of mine, *Mushroom Roulette*, was performed outdoors at the June Lake Theater Festival in June Lake, California. It felt satisfying to watch a play about a couple getting lost in the woods spring to life among the towering trees. Then came the year 2020, which brought an extraordinary shift in how we could enjoy each other's company and the arts. None of us knew how long indoor theaters would be closed, but many hoped that the show could go on *outside*, in 2021 and beyond. Inspired by my own experience with site-specific work and in an effort to continue creating and to elevate contemporary playwrights, I approached Applause Books about this collaboration. LineStorm Playwrights decided to contribute plays by members of our collective and to select other plays from a range of writers who captured the joy, fear, heartache, and humor of our time. Of course, these plays can be performed inside, on a traditional stage, and they can also be set in a backyard, on a front porch, in a park, by a pool, or under the stars.

This anthology is presented by LineStorm Playwrights, Oregon-based writers who read, critique, and produce each other's work. The group creates local festivals of new plays and supports members in their ongoing artistic process. As of 2021, the collective has fourteen members who write in a variety of formats—full-length plays, one-acts, theater for young audiences, spoken word, musical theater, opera, film, television, and more.

Many thanks to the experts and friends who read alongside us: Pierre Adeli, Nif Lindsay, Matt Pavik, Vivian Strange, and Charlotte

Ward. As always, we are grateful to Ronni Lacroute for a constant commitment to the arts. And special thanks to the whole LineStorm team: your wisdom and inventiveness are matched by your kindness and your desire to make and share new work.

Finally, thank you for reading and producing these plays. For exploring from the inner reaches of humanity to the vast universe around us. For getting lost in the woods and finding your way home. Now, go play outside!

—Lolly Ward

LineStorm Playwrights members, 2021:

Sara Jean Accuardi	E. M. Lewis
Alan Alexander III	Matthew Miller
Brianna Barrett	Anya Pearson
Audrey Block	Holly Yurth Richards
Susan Faust	Rich Rubin
Heath Hyun Houghton	Josie Seid
Dan Kitrosser	Lolly Ward

Lolly Ward's plays include *Mate* (The Actors' Gang; California Institute of Technology), *Do You Take This Woman?* (Smith & Kraus, *Best Ten Minute Plays of 2019*), and *Gone* (developed with The Inkwell Theater through the Max K. Lerner Playwriting Fellowship). She originated roles in Sarah Ruhl's *Orlando* and has served as a dramaturg and judge for Caltech's MACH 33 Festival of New Science-Driven Plays. As a member of The Actors' Gang, she toured nationally and internationally and acted in both the stage and film versions of *Embedded* at the Public Theater. After several years in Los Angeles as a member of the Playwrights Union, she moved to Portland, Oregon, where she cofounded and directs LineStorm Playwrights.

For more information, visit linestormplaywrights.com.

BREAK TIME

Desireé York

Desireé York is a writer/director whose plays include *The Puppeteer, One Second Chance, Undone, Fractured, Floating, Break Time, Human(e), In Your Dreams,* and *Hiding Out Loud.* She is a recipient of the 2015 Kennedy Center Rosa Parks Playwriting Award and recognized by Dayton Most Metro for the Best New Work of 2017–2018. Her work has been produced/developed/commissioned by Pasadena Playhouse/Caltech MACH 33 Festival, Detroit Repertory Theatre, the Garry Marshall Theatre, Dayton Playhouse, Breath of Fire Latina Theater Ensemble, Sacred Fools Theater Company, and Theatricum Botanicum, among others. Additionally, her plays have been finalists for the Ashland New Plays Festival, FutureFest, Henley Rose Playwright Competition, and semifinalists for the O'Neill National Playwrights Conference and CTG Humanitas Playwriting Prize. She is a member of the PlayGround-LA Writers Group, LAFPI, Honor Roll!, the Dramatists Guild of America, and serves as a mentor for WriteGirl. Website: desireeyork.com.

SYNOPSIS

Three nurses hope to escape life and death under an invisible tree with just a pack of cigarettes.

CHARACTERS

SHAWNA, late 20s, female.
ANNE, early 30s, female.
JESSE, 25 years old, female.

SETTING

Midsummer, in a sandlot across from a hospital.

TIME

Present day.

NOTE

In memory of Sandy.

Two nurses wearing scrubs come outside to take their break and find some shade while pulling out a pack of cigarettes.

SHAWNA: Hey.

JESSE: Hey. Damn, it's hot out here.

SHAWNA: That's why they took down that tree. They want you to take your breaks in the break room.

JESSE: Think they control the weather too?

SHAWNA: Control everything else. You lost your lighter?

JESSE: Left it at a friend's.

SHAWNA: Do I know this friend?

JESSE: No. It was a Tinder thing.

SHAWNA: Same one as last week?

JESSE: No, a different one. Can I use your lighter now?

(SHAWNA gives the lighter to JESSE.)

This new?

SHAWNA: Yeah. Derek gave it to me.

JESSE: I thought he wanted you to quit?

SHAWNA: Some kind of reverse psychology or something.

JESSE: Is it working?

(She hands the lighter back to SHAWNA, who takes a drag.)

SHAWNA: Does it look like it? How's things on the second floor?

JESSE: Mrs. Feldman died.

SHAWNA: What?! No.

JESSE: Took her vitals last night, went through the check list . . . she was talking about her geraniums and gardening shit. Couldn't wait to get her hands back in the dirt. Pretty ironic, don't you think?

(She laughs dryly.)

SHAWNA: I'm sorry, Jesse.

JESSE: Why?

SHAWNA: Didn't you say she reminded you of your grandma?

JESSE: Well, now they have one more thing in common. Great. Here comes Anne. I thought she was too good for us now she quit.

SHAWNA: Give her a break.

JESSE: Look, I get it, but I don't need to be lectured on how to do my job just because her . . .

(ANNE enters.)

ANNE: Didn't there used to be a tree out here?

JESSE: Its disappearance is part of a hospital conspiracy, according to Shawna.

ANNE: Is it really worth it? Walking out in this heat?

SHAWNA: Hey, I get my exercise and control my diet: killing two birds with one stone.

ANNE: "Killing" the operative word.

JESSE: You don't have to come.

ANNE: And miss all the fun? It's the only time I get to see you guys anymore, what with—

JESSE: Yeah, we know.

SHAWNA: How is Lily?

ANNE: She's all right. I mean, as good as you can be during chemo. Hey, you know that nurse practitioner with the super long nails, always has them painted some different color almost every freakin' day?

SHAWNA: Yeah?

ANNE: What do you think of her?

SHAWNA: I don't really know her, but she seems—

ANNE: (*Interrupting.*) Like a real B-I-T-C-H? Excuse my language.

SHAWNA: Really?

ANNE: Her bedside manner is atrocious. I mean, god forbid she take a moment and actually make eye contact with the patient.

JESSE: Maybe she's got other things on her mind.

ANNE: Yeah, but it's one thing to have something else on your mind and another to just act like a robot.

JESSE: We've all had our days.

ANNE: Are you her best friend or something?

SHAWNA: Isn't she a newbie?

ANNE: That's what I thought. She's a transfer, but she's been doing oncology for over ten years.

SHAWNA: It never gets any easier.

ANNE: I know, but I wish we could switch.

SHAWNA: Then switch.

ANNE: She's on the shift that works best with our schedule. And it's not that she doesn't do a good job, she just—

JESSE: (*Interrupting.*) Rubs you the wrong way.

ANNE: Exactly.

JESSE: You are such a . . .

ANNE: Excuse me?

SHAWNA: Hey now, let's not—

ANNE: (*Interrupting.*) No. Let her finish. I wanna hear her bullshit her way out of this one.

SHAWNA: Whoa. Since when do you curse?

ANNE: Since I quit smoking.

JESSE: She has the divine right now.

ANNE: So what's your problem? You don't like that I have standards?

JESSE: I don't have a problem. You're the one with the problem.

ANNE: Obviously. I have a six-year-old daughter with cancer.

SHAWNA: Can we please—

ANNE: (*Interrupting.*) Look, I know you think you know it all at twenty-five, but—

JESSE: (*Interrupting.*) You're not that much older than me, though you look about a hundred.

ANNE: Don't worry, you'll catch up real fast suckin' down those things.

SHAWNA: All right, all right, let's—

ANNE: (*Interrupting.*) You're as bad as that nurse practitioner.

JESSE: I do what it takes to survive.

ANNE: That's all you ever do: the bare minimum. Just enough to get by.

JESSE: At least I have the balls to look death in the face.

SHAWNA: Come on, this is our break.

ANNE: Break from what? No one gets a break from death. Sure, you can stave it off for a while but—

JESSE: (*Interrupting.*) Death always wins.

ANNE: You wanna tell that to my six-year-old? You got the "balls" to look her in the eyes and hook her up to that poison?

JESSE: (*She takes a final drag on her cigarette.*) She's your daughter, Anne. No one's ever gonna be good enough. Not even you.

(*She puts out her cigarette and goes to leave.*)

ANNE: (*She grabs JESSE's arm.*) Give me a cigarette.

SHAWNA: What? No, Anne. Let her go.

JESSE: Why don't you ask her?

ANNE: She won't give me one.

SHAWNA: You're sure as hell right I won't. And neither will she. Right, Jesse?

JESSE: I'm not her keeper.

(*She gets out a cigarette and gives it to ANNE.*)

SHAWNA: Yeah, well, I've got the lighter, so it's pretty useless.

ANNE: Come on, Shawna.

SHAWNA: No, Anne. You've come so far. I'm not gonna let you—

ANNE: (*Interrupting.*) Come so far for what? If you can tell me that, I'll never smoke again.

SHAWNA: This is crazy.

ANNE: Come on. What's the point, huh?

JESSE: Mrs. Feldman died last night.

ANNE: Shit. Really? I thought she was stable?

JESSE: She was when I took her vitals last night.

ANNE: Hey, you couldn't have known—

JESSE: (*Interrupting.*) I know.

ANNE: See?

(She leans toward SHAWNA to light her cigarette.)

JESSE: Give her a fuckin' light.

SHAWNA: You know what? Here you go!

(She chucks her cigarette and lighter onto the ground.)

Keep it. I'm through.

ANNE: Shawna?

SHAWNA: No, no more. I'm tired. I can't do this anymore. I quit.

ANNE: You can't quit.

JESSE: Shawna come on, it's no big deal.

SHAWNA: Maybe you can make jokes and laugh about all of this, but I can't. And Anne, you know I've always looked up to you, but now . . .

ANNE: Now I'm the bitch.

JESSE: You're trying to cope. Like we all are.

SHAWNA: Cope with what? Life or death?

ANNE: One doesn't exist without the other.

JESSE: Where is this coming from?

SHAWNA: What do you mean, "Where is this coming from?" Can't you see? Day after day it all ends the same. And then they take down the goddam tree? I should have stayed a philosophy major.

JESSE: Philosophers are pussies.

SHAWNA: Pussies?

ANNE: Yeah, no, she's right. They are. They never have to get their hands dirty like we do.

JESSE: I dated a philosophy professor once.

ANNE: Dated?

JESSE: All right, I hooked up with him. Terrible. I mean, the worst. Spent too much time in his head. Not enough hands-on experience.

SHAWNA: We're not talking about one of your sexual escapades, Jesse. I'm talking about real life.

JESSE: No, you're talking about your life. Don't blame me if you can't handle it.

SHAWNA: And you're handling it so much better? You never let yourself get attached to anyone.

JESSE: What's the point?

SHAWNA: That's what I'm saying! Why are we here, why do we even bother if it all turns out the same?

ANNE: Because until my daughter is dead, she's still living.

SHAWNA: Shit. Anne. I know. I'm sorry.

ANNE: It's okay. You just need time.

JESSE: We all need time.

(*Beat.*)

ANNE: You're scheduled to work a double this weekend, aren't you?

SHAWNA: Yeah.

JESSE: I'll take it.

SHAWNA: I can't ask you to do that.

ANNE: We'll split it.

SHAWNA: Anne, no—

ANNE: (*Interrupting.*) I think a cigarette should seal the deal.

JESSE: She's earned it, Shawna. So have you.

> (*She sifts the lighter out of the sand and hands it to SHAWNA. They all light up and take a deep drag.*)

ANNE: When's your shift over?

SHAWNA: Same as yesterday.

JESSE: Let's grab Starbucks.

ANNE: Lily has chemo.

JESSE: Then I'll get to meet the manicured bitch.

ANNE: (*She chuckles, takes another drag and exhales.*) God. I forgot how nice it is out here.

SHAWNA: I think it was a sycamore.

ANNE: I think you're right. That's probably why they took it down.

JESSE: Oh yeah, I remember now. Maintenance was always bitching about how messy it was.

ANNE: Messy in a beautiful way.

SHAWNA: (*She looks at her watch.*) Hey. Break's over.

> (*They all take a final drag, stamp out their cigarettes and look up, remembering where the tree used to be. They exit.*)

END OF PLAY

BUTTERFLIES EAT DECAY

Anya Pearson

Anya Pearson is an award-winning playwright, poet, producer, actress, and activist. She is on staff at Corporeal Writing and is a 2021–2022 Hodder Fellow at Princeton University. Anya is currently finishing her debut collection of poetry, *This Is the After*, writing television pilots, and constantly plotting, planning, devising, creating, imagining, and revising visions of a better, more just world. Her plays include *The Measure of Innocence* (The Kilroys List, Drammy Award for Best Original Script, finalist: Oregon Book Award for Drama), *Made to Dance in Burning Buildings* (Showcase: Joe's Pub, New York City; Shaking the Tree, Portland, Oregon), *The Killing Fields* (2018 Orphic Commission; Seven Devils; GPTC; VTC), and *Three Love Songs* (Play at Home initiative, Portland Center Stage). Memberships: LineStorm Playwrights, the Dramatists Guild, Couch Film Collective, Actors' Equity Association. Website: anyapearson.com.

SYNOPSIS

A modern love story.
Or not.
You decide.

CHARACTERS

HER
HIM

NOTE

The roles of Her and Him can be performed by anyone.
Any age, any gender identity, any ethnicity, any sexual orientation.

PART ONE: YESTERDAY

HIM: I had a dream last night. About you.

HER: I dreamt of you again last night.

HIM: I wanted to call you . . .

HER: Again.

HIM: I am going to call you.

HER AND HIM: Without you

HIM: my shoulders are stiff

HER: my throat is hot

HIM: my hands feel like jelly

HER: my stomach is distended

HER AND HIM: Without you, life is

HIM: rancid

HER: frantic

HIM: Without you

HER: Without you
  is taut shoulders
  the get-away-from-me lodged in my frown
  Pushing everyone away for their not-you-ness

HIM: Without you
  is late nights
  all the late nights
  the brain spins
  and stomach drops.
  Interrogating the ceiling.
  Stalking you on Instagram.

HER: Endless lists of things
  not being done
  Should be
  being done
  not being done.
  The lists of
  if I do this,
  win this,
  get this,
  will he notice?

HIM: this endless lack of sleep

HER: Sad songs on repeat

HIM: How much will this cost me tomorrow . . .
  Getting swallowed in the creases of the bed where you should be.

HER: being on fucking dating sites

HIM: being on dating sites during a fucking pandemic
  Without you

HER: is the opening of the door,

HIM: the slamming shut,
the start, the surge, the panic—the feeling of impending doom

HER: Without you is
feeling the need to immortalize you again
And again
And again
And even when you do not deserve it.

HIM: Without you is
fatigue
being nauseated by the mundane.
Exhausted by people who bleed mediocrity.

HER: friendships that do not satisfy my need to be seen

HIM: Loneliness.

HER: Longing.

HIM: longing.

HER: loneliness.

HIM: is the ache of wanting

HER: and never finding

HIM: It's an ache
in the gut
that refuses to be silenced

HER: A rumble

HIM: A gurgle

HER: An interruption

HIM: A warning signal

HER: It's an acid wash to the chest because . . .
    that place in my breastbone that is hollow
    Never filled
    Never satisfied
    Never sure how to artfully navigate this you-shaped hole

    It's the tint of dismal on a sunny day
    The way people say, it's gorgeous outside, did you see?
    But all I see is the gray in the blue sky

HIM: It's the salt on the tongue that other people register as sugar
    Or when we were kids
    and we used to dare each other to eat Kool-Aid raw
    To burn our tongues
    Knowing even then that pain could be better
    When we metered it out on our own terms.
    Under our own construction.

HER: It's the stiffness in my neck that will not settle
    It's the sharp pain that crops up in my left breast

HIM: In my right foot
    on the outside near my ankle

HER: In my hands

HIM: In my knuckles

HER: In my belly
    It always goes back to the belly
    this memory of desire.

HIM: The memory of it

HER: is a cloud in haze

HIM: A sense that I should know this, but I don't
    It is the part of me that wants people
    to find me desirable (wants you to)

HER: That wants to know what
  to say to myself when I need soothing

HIM: It's the idea that I should have eaten long ago, but I am still
  starving

HER: Is it wanting and not wanting
  to be disappointed
  The idea that your want
  can be fulfilled

HIM: That is the scary part of desire
  Sitting in the unknown
  Sitting in that pool of disappointment
  when you do have the courage to reach
  with desire

HER: And instead you are smacked with disappointment

HIM: You are familiar

HER: With your aloneness
  Your differentness
  Your sense of all that is not there
  Desire is a pang just the side opposite of hunger

HIM: You are formidable

HER: Neither of them ever soothable
  Neither of them ever fillable.

HIM: You are
  my forever.

HER: My story of love

HIM: Is you.

PART TWO: TODAY

HIM: I had a dream last night. About you.

HER: I dreamt of you again last night. Again.

HIM: I was going to call . . .

HER: My heart fluttered.

HIM: I wanted to know how you were doing. I wanted to call but—

HER: My story of love is still you.

HIM: I don't know. I get scared.
　　I don't think I could actually tell you that though.

HER: Someone—I am not sure if it is me or you—but someone in this
　　story is wholly unreliable as a narrator.

HIM: Maybe it is the actual tether between us . . .

HER: that is faulty in its construction.

HIM: When I woke up, I wanted to call. I just—

HER: My story of love is still you.

HIM: I . . . when I talk to you—I get so nervous—
　　I have to be the biggest, boldest version of myself. I have to live
　　up to what I think you want or need. Because I am afraid that
　　you won't like the quiet version of me.

HER: You are messing up my life. You know in the movies when they
　　have the big fight and then somehow that makes them realize
　　how much they love each other? I wanted that. I wanted to yell
　　and scream and tell you that.

HIM: My story of love is still you.

HER: There is something in getting you to see me that feels vital to my
　　survival.

HIM: I was afraid to call.

HER: The silly thing—

HIM: You scare me. Always have. I am scared of how much I need you.

HER: The silly thing—the really messed up thing—is that you have never seen me. You have never bothered to see what was right in front of you.

HIM: There is something in me that feels unsettled around you. And I need you to know—I cannot deal with how that makes me feel. I just—can't be—can't think—can't overcome the way you unsettle me.

HER: This is the hardest but truest love story. For myself.

HIM: You deserve someone who isn't afraid.

HER: You are not for me.

HIM: I have worked my ass to get where I am, and I deserve to be proud. I come from nothing, you know that. My dad is somewhere right now sleeping in an alley. That's what I come from. And look at me now. Look at what I have done. Who I have become.
And I can't let anything or anyone get in the way of what I have built. Even you.

HER: I deserve someone better than you . . . I deserve . . . this just feels like words. It feels like the thing you say to keep from drinking—keep from binging junk food—stuffing the yearning with sugar and salt, soothing the lonely with bullshit affirmations. "I deserve someone who will really see me." I pretend that this is helping—but it is not. The salve that doesn't stop the bleeding, does not cure the infection, does not reattach the severed limbs.

HIM: I am going to call you . . .

HER: But I go through the motions and pretend anyway.

HIM: I didn't call.

PART THREE: TOMORROW

HER: I had a dream last night. You were there. Again.

It was one of those dreams where it's real . . . but not real, you know? Like . . . you know it's you, but maybe you look different than you normally do . . . or you're flying through the sky . . . or the walls are made of Jell-O.

The Jell-O walls are a metaphor, obviously. But I don't really know for what. Not yet. Maybe I never will.

You know the liminal space—that half-truth, half-zany, half-reality, half-what is up with my subconscious and how I am supposed to decipher this—that type of dream space?

But you, no matter how insane the backdrop—Jell-O walls, human butterflies, teeth falling out—no matter what the set of circumstances—you are always clear. I can feel you in my dreams, then I have to remind myself when I wake up that you aren't really there.

Do you ever feel like your dreams are trying to tell you something? Like they want to help you figure your shit out, right?

Maybe you're the Jell-O I'm stuck in. Maybe you're the teeth that keep falling out of my mouth.

Anyway, you were there. You looked a little different than your real self—but the feeling—I knew it was you because of the feeling. The feeling of you is undeniable.

You know those dreams where you are fighting but your arms don't work? You, like, have noodle arms for some reason. You ever get those? It was like that.

In the dream, you were dying. You were literally wasting away before my eyes, and I wanted to save you. I was trying desperately to save you, but I couldn't. I couldn't save you because of the noodle arms.

The subconscious is a trip. The way the subconscious sends us messages is so coded and weird and hard to detangle. Sometimes I wish I could say, look, Brain—can you just say what you came to say? What do you think I am doing wrong? And what do you want me to do about it?

But then it hits me . . . thank you, Subconscious—I suddenly knew that the only way I could save you was to sacrifice myself. You know, like, go in your place, to whatever afterlife you were headed to.

I was ready to do it.

What does that say though?

But I had those freaking noodle arms, and I couldn't move. So I just stood there on the side of the bank watching you sink into quicksand. I watched you slowly sink, and I thought—I need to help him. But I couldn't. Part of me . . . wouldn't. Maybe part of me knew that I shouldn't.

Someone told me the other day about the dark side of butterflies. They eat decay. There's something in that—what's underneath the story that most people tell. Most people just see the beauty, bright colors, pretty wings, an uplifting metaphor about transformation. Most people ignore the decay and the darkness and the violence that leads to that hard-fought beauty.

END OF PLAY

CAMPING TRIP

Emilie Landmann

Emilie Landmann's most notable work, *Matthew McConaughey vs. The Devil: An American Myth*, was an official selection of the 2017 New York Musical Festival Next Link Project. The musical was nominated for several awards of excellence, including Best Musical and Best Book. Her latest play, *Stop! (motion)*, premiered digitally with The Broken Planetarium for the 2021 Fertile Ground Festival. Emilie has worked as a director, playwright, and actor in the Portland, Oregon, area for several years. Companies she has worked with include: Enlightened Theatrics, Theatre Vertigo, Action/Adventure Theatre, Experience Theatre Project, Portland Actors Ensemble, Profile Theatre, Post5 Theatre, Portland Civic Theatre Guild, and Portland Playhouse.

SYNOPSIS

The camping trip of two adult sisters is thrown into chaos when a young hiker offering psychedelics crashes the party.

CHARACTERS

MEGAN, a woman in her mid- to late 30s.
VANESSA, Megan's older sister, late 30s.
JUSTIN, a 24-year-old man hiking the Pacific Coast Trail.

SETTING

A quiet campsite somewhere on Mount Hood.

TIME

Summer.

JUSTIN sits frozen in a camping chair next to a fire pit and cooler. A sleeping bag lies nearby. MEGAN enters lugging two jugs of water. She freezes when she sees JUSTIN. She looks around and hesitantly approaches.

MEGAN: Hi . . . That's my camping chair . . . I don't know what you're doing or what you want, but my sister and I reserved this spot weeks ago . . . Vanessa! Hey, Vanessa!

(The sleeping bag stirs; VANESSA pops her head out and sits up in it.)

VANESSA: (*Giggling.*) Megan! Megan, look! I'm a caterpillar. The very hungry caterpillar.

(MEGAN crouches down by VANESSA, who grabs a water jug and chugs. JUSTIN still hasn't moved.)

MEGAN: Why is there a stranger in my camping chair?

VANESSA: Yeah, that's Justin—

JUSTIN: I am Justin.

MEGAN: I don't feel comfortable with this guy—

VANESSA: He's cool. He was hiking through, and I invited him to take a rest here. Oh my God, this water must be from the spring of the gods. It's delicious.

MEGAN: Something seems off about him—

VANESSA: He's coming down from a trip.

MEGAN: From Mount Hood?

JUSTIN: From myself.

MEGAN: . . . Are you high?

VANESSA: I had my first shroom, don't tell Mom. At first, I was anxious, but now I'm a hungry caterpillar.

(VANESSA tries biting MEGAN but is limited in her mobility due to the sleeping bag.)

JUSTIN: I'd offer you some, but I gave Vanessa my last cap.

MEGAN: I was gone for just over an hour! How could you do this?!

VANESSA: It was a very long hour.

JUSTIN: Time is a social construct.

VANESSA: Megan, we need to trip at home. You can feel the universe hugging you.

MEGAN: No, because I have children, and so do you. As well as a husband whom you love.

VANESSA: Nope. Not this caterpillar.

MEGAN: This is my one weekend away from the kids, Vanessa. You knew that. Now I have to babysit you. Fantastic. What a great sisters' bonding experience.

VANESSA: Don't worry about me. I am WELL. We can still bond. We have so much time to do that now.

MEGAN: We only have one day—

VANESSA: No, we have a lifetime, because I got let go last week. So, I have nothing going on!

MEGAN: Holy shit, Vanessa.

VANESSA: No, it's all good. The universe is smiling at me. Life is awesome.

MEGAN: Are you at least getting a severance package?

VANESSA: Shhh. This is vibe time. Not worry time. Remember? We aren't moms this weekend. You can be Fun Megan again, like in college.

MEGAN: I'm fun. I'm the classroom mom who always has Jolly Ranchers.

VANESSA: Jolly Ranchers are not fun.

MEGAN: I never stopped being fun. I AM Fun Megan!

(MEGAN grabs a beer from the cooler and shotguns it. She has obviously not shotgunned a beer in over a decade. She powers through. VANESSA hops around like a rabbit in her sleeping bag.)

VANESSA: Yes! We are having so much fun on our camping trip! Woo!

JUSTIN: You two are a hoot!

(VANESSA falls exhausted to the ground.)

VANESSA: I never wanted to work in exports anyway. Do you know any kids who dream of working for a customs broker? When I was a kid, I wanted to be a ballerina.

MEGAN: I wanted to be a teacher.

VANESSA: Boring! You never let yourself dream big!

JUSTIN: I wanted to be a stay-at-home dad.

MEGAN: Aw. That's actually really nice. What do you do now?

JUSTIN: I live. I eat. I breathe. I love. I am. That's what I do.

MEGAN: But for money?

JUSTIN: Oh, I have a trust fund.

MEGAN: You are so lucky.

JUSTIN: I've been hiking the Pacific Coast Trail for the past four months—

MEGAN: I saw *Wild* with Reese Witherspoon. I know you need a crapload of gear, a big backpack and all. Where's the backpack?

JUSTIN: Huh. I must have left it somewhere on the trail here.

MEGAN: You're not worried someone is going to steal it?

JUSTIN: I trust in the goodness of mankind, and in return, goodness is returned to me. So, no, I'm not worried.

MEGAN: Ah, to be young and worry-free again. Wait 'til you become a parent. What are you, twenty-three? Twenty-four?

JUSTIN: According to the Gregorian calendar, I'm twenty-four. But I met a psychic in the redwoods who told me my soul was actually one hundred and ten years old.

VANESSA: I love that. An old soul. I'm only old in age. My hair is getting gray, I have stretch marks, and I need eye cream. Only old ladies need eye cream.

JUSTIN: Does anyone need eye cream? Or is that all capitalism?

VANESSA: Oh man. I DON'T need eye cream. I don't need a job. I don't need anything but the sun and the earth. Wow. Oh wow. I've had a huge breakthrough. Megan, I need to tell you something. This is important, I want to stay here. In the wilderness. Sleeping on the dirt. Gathering food like a squirrel. Wandering around like the nomads do. Oh no, that's offensive.

MEGAN: Nomad isn't an offensive term.

VANESSA: Are you sure?

JUSTIN: I think it's pretty offensive. I think they prefer the term "land mammals."

MEGAN: Where did you get that— Forget it. Vanessa, you don't want to live out here forever. You are high.

VANESSA: No, I'm finally awake. I see the world as it really is. This is what I want. I think I've wanted it for a long time, I've just never known.

MEGAN: What are you going to tell Dan? What about Maeve and Toby? You're abandoning them to be a nomad?

JUSTIN: Land mammal. She's a land mammal now.

VANESSA: I'm serious, Megan. Maybe I'll get a van, and a dog. Or a yurt.

JUSTIN: I know a guy who's looking to sell a van. I'll give you his number.

MEGAN: You are not buying a van. You are going to come down, realize how stupid everything is, and we will go on being boring old ladies again.

VANESSA: No! I will be Fun Vanessa from now on! This is a time in my life for metamorphosis. Besides, Dan and I are separated anyway.

MEGAN: You have got to be kidding me.

VANESSA: Nope. For, like, three months now.

MEGAN: You never thought to tell me that?

VANESSA: I'm telling you now.

MEGAN: Oh, yes. This is a perfect time. Just you, me, the drugs, and a complete stranger.

VANESSA: This is why I don't tell you things. Because you get mean and judgy. Remember Fun Megan? Where'd she go?

MEGAN: I don't want to be Fun Megan; I want you to tell me what the hell is going on with your life!

VANESSA: No! I'm moving to the woods, and you'll never hear from me again!

MEGAN: I am far too sober to be dealing with this level of insanity right now.

(MEGAN grabs another beer.)

VANESSA: I have a plan. I'll write a letter to Dan and the kids explaining my metamorphosis. Justin invited me to hike with him to Canada, so we'll do that, and after that I'll use my savings to buy us a van!

MEGAN: You've just met this guy.

VANESSA: Justin is free and open, and accepts me for who I am. He hasn't once judged me.

JUSTIN: I radically accept everyone as they are.

VANESSA: I need you to radically accept me and my life choices, Megan. Honestly, this short but significant connection I've had with Justin is more than I've ever had with Dan.

MEGAN: You'd have a connection with a ham sandwich if it gave you an ounce of attention.

VANESSA: See! There! You are a mean person.

MEGAN: You want me to be mean?! I'll show you how mean I can be!

(MEGAN gets on top of VANESSA in the sleeping bag and starts hitting her.)

This is me being mean! And I'm having so much fun doing it!

VANESSA: Stop it! Stop! You are a jerk!

MEGAN: No, I'm not! You're immature!

VANESSA: You're boring!

MEGAN: I'm trying to stop you from ruining your life!

VANESSA: You have no life!

MEGAN: At least I can keep a husband and a job!

(Pause.)

VANESSA: Too far.

MEGAN: I'm sorry. I didn't mean—

VANESSA: I am so ready to be away from all of this negativity.

(A moment passes. JUSTIN gets up from the chair and stretches, startling VANESSA and MEGAN.)

JUSTIN: I think . . . Yeah, I'm pretty much lucid now. Wow, that was a good one. I'd hang out, but I gotta go if I want to reach my next stop by sundown.

VANESSA: Are we leaving? I can grab my gear!

JUSTIN: You are very nice, and I had a wonderful trip with you, but I need to do this alone.

VANESSA: But you understand me, you GET me. You INVITED me!

JUSTIN: Did I? Sorry, I get way too familiar with people when I trip. I have issues with boundaries. . . . Man, I'm so awkward with goodbyes. Have a good one!

(JUSTIN exits.)

VANESSA: Wait! Justin! Don't leave yet! Please! I want to be free like you!

(VANESSA struggles to get out of her sleeping bag. By the time she is out it is too late, and JUSTIN is gone. VANESSA slowly gets back into her sleeping bag, making herself a cocoon. A moment passes. MEGAN grabs two beers from the cooler and sits next to the sleeping bag cocoon.)

MEGAN: I'm sorry about everything I said— It's only because I was angry and day-drunk.

VANESSA: You are always angry.

MEGAN: Of course, I am. Have you met my kids? The amount of learning and attention disorders they have is scary.

VANESSA: You know they got it from you.

MEGAN: I know! Trust me. I know.

VANESSA: I don't want to be me anymore. I want to be a twenty-four-year-old with time and a trust fund.

MEGAN: Me too. Me too.

VANESSA: *(Peeking her head out of the cocoon.)* I was going to tell you everything. I swear. It's so embarrassing.

MEGAN: Do you want to talk about it now?

VANESSA: Not while the trees are moving the way they are. I'm still tripping. Do you think I'm an idiot?

MEGAN: (*Trying to be as nice as she can.*) I think you were very easily influenced by outside substances. But the good thing is that we are alone here. No witnesses. It'll be our secret.

VANESSA: Remember when I was a caterpillar? I was so happy then. I'm just a lump of goo now.

MEGAN: You could turn into a butterfly. Metamorphosis.

VANESSA: A monarch. I've always looked good in orange. I'll fly south for the winter. A nomad butterfly.

MEGAN: I think you mean a land mammal.

VANESSA: I don't get it.

MEGAN: Me neither.

> (*MEGAN hands VANESSA a beer. They drink together as they watch the trees move.*)

END OF PLAY

CLOUD ILLUSIONS

Susan Faust

Susan Faust is an Oregon-based playwright and director whose background is in devised theater. Her play *Confabulous* was a finalist for the 2020 Portland Civic Theatre Guild New Play Award, and her one-act *Strangest Yellow* was published in the *Silk Road Review*. Susan was a founding member of the San Francisco-based Paducah Mining Company and has collaborated with Anne Bogart's internationally renowned SITI Company and with Portland's Hand2Mouth Theatre. She has been a playwright-in-residence with Portland Public Schools and a playwriting mentor for at-risk youth with Haven Project. Susan is a cofounder of LineStorm Playwrights and is a member of the Dramatists Guild.

SYNOPSIS

When two strangers meet on Hampstead Heath during a gathering of the Cloud Appreciation Society, unusual sightings are made, personal stories are shared, and the rain comes down.

CHARACTERS

NADEEM, 30s, male, British Indian, currently living in Bristol.
IMOGEN, 70s, female, any race, native Londoner.

SETTING

The play takes place on top of Parliament Hill in Hampstead Heath, London.

TIME

Now.

NADEEM enters and surveys the scene, looking around for something . . . someone. He wanders from one area to another and eventually sits on an empty bench facing the London skyline (and the audience). Taking a pre-packed sandwich from a small bag, he removes it from its plastic container and takes a bite as he looks out over London. After a moment, he takes a photo out of his wallet. The hint of a smile forms on his face as he gazes at the photo.

IMOGEN enters, holding a large bag full of who knows what.

IMOGEN: Thank heavens, a place to sit. Look at that sky! There are cloudy skies and there are skies full of clouds—and you'd best know the difference, isn't that right?!

NADEEM: Sorry?

IMOGEN: Of course the real question is: Will there be any rare or unusual sightings?

    (She sits down on the bench next to NADEEM.)

Ah! I believe there's a mermaid among us. Do you see her? Right up there, swimming towards the waterfall. I do hope she knows what's coming!

(She laughs heartily, then looks over at NADEEM.)

Oh, my. What have we here? Another amateur cloud spotter?

(NADEEM moves over to make space between them.)

NADEEM: What makes you think that?

IMOGEN: You mustn't be shy about it.

NADEEM: Perhaps you've mistaken me for someone else.

IMOGEN: You're here, aren't you? Must be your first time!

NADEEM: Uh . . .

IMOGEN: Good for you. That's the first step, isn't it? Acknowledging who you are!

NADEEM: I'm sorry . . . ?

IMOGEN: Believe me, I've been at it so long I have a second sense about these things.

NADEEM: Right . . .

IMOGEN: Sometimes I'm on the bus and I see someone looking out the window. Not a casual look, mind you. No, more a gaze of longing. Searching for the evocative, the poetic—the promise of a simpler world. That's what we're all looking for, isn't it? Some of us are just keener than others.

(She smiles.)

You're one of us.

(NADEEM gathers his things and gets up to leave.)

NADEEM: I'll leave you to it.

IMOGEN: Oh, dear, I've frightened you off, have I?

NADEEM: No, no . . . I've just got to head home.

IMOGEN: Well, for goodness' sake, sit down and finish your lunch first.

> (*NADEEM looks at the sandwich in his hands and sits back down. Awkward silence as he eats. IMOGEN picks NADEEM's photo off the ground and hands it to him.*)

I think you dropped this.

NADEEM: Oh! Thank you.

> (*He takes the photo and hastily puts it back into his wallet.*)

IMOGEN: Is that your child?

> (*Silence.*)

The photograph?

NADEEM: Yes.

IMOGEN: How old?

NADEEM: He's . . . almost fourteen now.

IMOGEN: Oh, I see! Well, you must get a more recent picture for your wallet then, mustn't you?!

> (*She laughs.*)

We never had children, Nigel and I. He used to say the plants were our children. I used to say the garden was his mistress. So many beautiful days he spent tending to her while I languished with only a book for company!

> (*Beat.*)

Such a lovely garden. Until the weeds took over. But then, you see, we both had clouds. A much more egalitarian pleasure. Of course you already know that, seeing as you're here.

NADEEM: Actually, I—

IMOGEN: C-A-S is such a varied group of people, really, you never tire of meeting new members.

NADEEM: I'm not a member of—

IMOGEN: Not to worry if you haven't joined yet. Anyone can come try it out before paying dues.

(*NADEEM gets up from the bench.*)

NADEEM: (*Practically shouting.*) I'm sorry, but I have absolutely no idea what you're going on about!

IMOGEN: I do apologize. I seem to have upset you.

(*Beat.*)

You're not here for the Cloud Appreciation Society meeting, then?

NADEEM: I haven't the faintest idea what that is.

(*Awkward pause.*)

Clouds are just water droplets, after all.

IMOGEN: (*Offended.*) And ice crystals.

(*Beat.*)

NADEEM: I suppose I have wondered what these dark storm clouds are called . . .

IMOGEN: Bosh! Alto–nimbo–strato–cumulus; don't be bothered by all those words! You can feel when it's going to rain, can't you? You don't need a scientist to tell you that. No, I'm here for the infinitely more subtle art of cloud interpretation.

(A moment.)

Well, then? What do you see?

NADEEM: Oh, you mean for me to try and—

IMOGEN: Of course!

(A long moment as NADEEM ponders the sky.)

Have you found anything?

NADEEM: Perhaps, a tiger . . .

IMOGEN: Where?

NADEEM: *(Pointing.)* Up there, crouching in the grass.

IMOGEN: Yes, indeed!

(She watches NADEEM looking up at the sky, then looks for herself.)

Oh look, Nigel! There's a cub to the east.

NADEEM: Right, I see the cub as well. My name is Nadeem, by the way.

IMOGEN: Pardon me.

NADEEM: And your name?

IMOGEN: Imogen.

(Beat.)

I lost Nigel, my husband, just over a year ago.

NADEEM: I'm very sorry. You must miss him.

IMOGEN: He loved to look at the clouds. It was about the only thing he could do at the end. I'd adjust his wheelchair into a reclining

position and take him out to the back garden. I'm not much of a
gardener, so the weeds had completely taken over by then. But Nigel
didn't take notice of the plants because he was aimed up at the sky!

(She laughs cheekily.)

What a time we had in the back garden together. He couldn't speak
those last few months, but whenever he spotted something up there,
he'd make a sound or shift in his chair, and I'd look for it as well.
Sometimes I got it wrong at first—and he'd let me know! But I would
always keep looking until I saw what Nigel saw.

*(It's quiet for a moment, as IMOGEN is caught up in her reverie.
Then the rain comes. Only a shower at first.)*

There we are, then. Out with the brollies!

*(IMOGEN takes an umbrella out of her bag and opens it. She looks
at NADEEM.)*

What, you haven't got yours?

NADEEM: It's back home in Bristol. But I don't mind the rain.

IMOGEN: Bristol's a bit of a journey. What brought you all the way to
London?

NADEEM: We used to live here.

IMOGEN: Hampstead's such a lovely corner of London.

NADEEM: We were in Islington. But we often came to the Heath on
Sundays. My son loved to fly his kite here.

IMOGEN: It's the perfect place to fly a kite. I suppose he's outgrown
that now. More interested in girls, no doubt!

(Silence.)

Perhaps you and your son would be interested in becoming members of the Cloud Appreciation Society. I'm sure you'd find plenty of events in Bristol. There are members all over Britain—all over the world, in fact.

(A moment.)

If you like, I can give you the information to—

NADEEM: I should probably get back to the railway station.

(The shower becomes pouring rain.)

IMOGEN: Come on, then. There's room under this brolly for two.

(NADEEM hesitates before going back to the bench and sitting close to IMOGEN, under her umbrella. IMOGEN pulls a package of jam tarts from her bag.)

Jam tart?

NADEEM: You have everything in that bag, don't you?

IMOGEN: (*Laughing.*) Just about. Take one.

NADEEM: No, thank you.

IMOGEN: Take the package with you then. You can eat them on the journey home or give them to—

NADEEM: I live alone now.

IMOGEN: Oh, I'm sorry.

(Beat.)

NADEEM: He's why I came, actually. My son, Ivaan—he disappeared when he was nine.

IMOGEN: Oh, no! How awful.

NADEEM: The police weren't very helpful. My wife and I paid a private investigator to look for him, but we ran out of money after two years. That's when my wife went back to her family in India . . . and I moved to Bristol.

(Beat.)

But I still keep hoping.

IMOGEN: No one should have to suffer what you have.

(Silence.)

NADEEM: Sometimes when I come up here, I wonder if he's ever been back to fly a kite. I know that sounds foolish. He could be anywhere.

(Beat.)

If he's still . . .

IMOGEN: It's not foolish at all.

NADEEM: Maybe I am searching for the poetic.

IMOGEN: I think you found it earlier. The tiger and cub—both fierce and full of grace.

(Beat.)

Ah, it stopped raining!

NADEEM: So it did.

(IMOGEN puts her umbrella away.)

IMOGEN: And would you look at that!

NADEEM: Oh!

IMOGEN: Magnificent.

NADEEM: It is, isn't it?

(They sit, looking up into the sky together.)

END OF PLAY

EPIC LOVE

Jami Brandli

Jami Brandli's plays include *Technicolor Life, S.O.E., M-Theory, The Caregiver's Guide, Sisters Three, Through the Eye of a Needle, Medusa's Song, O: A Rhapsody in Divorce,* and *BLISS (or Emily Post Is Dead!)*—named on The Kilroys List, an *LA Times* Critics' Choice, and nominated for Best Playwriting for an Original Play by the Los Angeles Ovation Awards. Her work has been produced/developed at New Dramatists, New York Theatre Workshop, The Road Theatre Company, The Women's Voices Theater Festival, LAUNCH PAD, Moving Arts, The Inkwell Theater, among other venues. Selected awards: John Gassner Memorial Playwriting Award, Holland New Voices Award, Ashland New Plays Festival, Aurora Theatre Company's GAP Prize, 2019 Humanitas Prize PLAY LA winner. Jami teaches dramatic writing at Lesley University's low-residency MFA program and is represented by the Michael Moore Agency and MSW Media Management. Website: jamibrandli.com.

SYNOPSIS

A married couple have their last date at their special spot in the woods.

CHARACTERS

PAT, female, early 60s to early 70s, any ethnicity. Chris' wife.
CHRIS, male, early 60s to early 70s, any ethnicity. Pat's husband.

SETTING

A car parked in a secluded wooded area.

TIME

Present day, evening.

NOTE

Epic Love can be performed outdoors or indoors.

A car (or two chairs on stage) with an open roof parked in a secluded wooded area. It's evening, and the night sky is filled with stars.

In the back of the car, CHRIS and PAT bask in the glow of postcoitus. And this round of lovemaking was, to be blunt, fucking incredible.

CHRIS: Wow. That was—

PAT: Tremendous.

CHRIS: Monumental.

PAT: Mind-blowing.

CHRIS: Epic.

PAT: That's the right word. Epic. *Epic* back-seat-of-a-car lovemaking.

CHRIS: Did I . . . Did I hurt you?

PAT: Didn't you just hear what I said?

CHRIS: I know, but . . . I just wanted to make sure I didn't hurt you.

PAT: What does it matter now?

CHRIS: It matters if I hurt you—

PAT: What matters is that it *did* happen. I was really worried that maybe I wouldn't be able to, but it was like my animalistic instincts kicked in and I just had to, I don't know, *devour* you.

CHRIS: I felt that. And I also felt you give me every piece of you. It was perfect.

(PAT reaches over and touches CHRIS' face.)

PAT: Yes. It was. Last times have to be perfection.

(A shift in the mood. PAT is resolved. CHRIS gets anxious, but he tries to hide it. PAT looks through the open roof at the stars in the night sky.)

The stars sure are vibrant tonight. It's as if they know why we're here. (*Beat.*) So, Chris. Do you have any regrets?

CHRIS: You want to talk about regrets?

PAT: Well, now's your chance.

CHRIS: I don't want to talk about regrets—

PAT: Okay. Then I'll start. I regret cheating on you.

CHRIS: You cheated on me?

PAT: Yes. In retaliation against you cheating on me.

CHRIS: Pat. I really don't want to talk about—

PAT: But *I* do. This is our last date, which, I want to say again, is also perfection. Coming here, to our spot, is just magic. I'm beyond grateful because I know this must be . . . difficult. BUT. I have to get this off my chest. I was so mad at you for risking our marriage for a fuck twenty years ago. So I said to myself, *Fuck it. I'll risk it, too.* And let me tell you something, that was the worst fuck of my life. So, I'm sorry. And now I can finally forgive myself for that god-awful fuck.

(Slight beat.)

CHRIS: Who was it?

PAT: You do *not* want to know. Trust me. So. Any regrets?

CHRIS: Cheating on you of course. And not kissing you on our first date.

PAT: You kissed me on our first date. Which was right here. And I also put out.

CHRIS: Well, on what *I* consider to be our first date, me kissing you did not happen.

PAT: (*A smile.*) How can you consider the party that our mutual friends threw together specifically for us to meet to be our first *date*? That was an introduction.

CHRIS: But we did stand very close to each other on the balcony, talking for hours and looking up at the stars.

PAT: And you trying to be all smooth. Telling me stories about the Andromeda and Perseus constellations.

CHRIS: And then we saw a shooting star at the same time, which of course was a sign. I turned to you and said, "You know what that means, right?" And then you replied, "Shooting stars mean nothing. They're as common as space dust."

PAT: Yikes. Talk about me killing the mood. And you still wanted to kiss me after that?

CHRIS: Are you kidding? I fell in love with you that night.

PAT: I fell in love with you—I think it was two months later—when you drove to my apartment and fixed my flat tire at six in the morning so I could get to work on time.

CHRIS: It was also pouring rain, by the way.

PAT: I knew right then that you were for me. My Chris.

CHRIS: Flaws aside.

PAT: All of our flaws aside now. (*Beat.*) I think what we had together was a great love. An *epic* love. Not everybody can say they had a marriage that survived for nearly forty years.

CHRIS: Thirty-eight years, six months, and two days to be exact.

(*PAT becomes more resolved and, at the same time, she seems to be fighting fatigue. CHRIS starts to lose his composure.*)

PAT: I'm proud of us, Chris. For weathering all of our storms and sticking by each other's side so we could have this epic love—

CHRIS: Pat—

PAT: And on top of that, we have one great kid who is healthy—

CHRIS: Pat, please—

PAT: *And* happy with a love of her own and a child *finally* on the way—

CHRIS: Jesus Christ—

PAT: Our epic grandchild is finally—

CHRIS: I can't do this! Okay? Goddammit, I CANNOT DO THIS.

(Slight beat.)

PAT: You have to. You promised.

CHRIS: I know I promised, but I can't. I want more days with you, more *months* and even another year if I can get it—

PAT: I don't have another *day* in me. You know this—

CHRIS: How about a compromise then? Six months of experimental trials and juice diets, and I'll find a shaman or something—

PAT: No—

CHRIS: Six months. Please. Just give me six months to find a miracle—

PAT: It was a miracle I survived the first time and certainly a goddam impossibility that I went into remission the second time!

CHRIS: Because you are a fighter who can survive anything! *We* can survive anything working together—!

PAT: Goddammit, Chris! I don't want to go over this *again*. There are no miracles left. But I am keeping my dignity and going out on *my* terms. *(Slight beat.)* Besides. I already took half of the pills.

CHRIS: You what? How—?

PAT: It doesn't matter how! I took half of them, and I want to take the other half *now*. I'm getting sleepy, so give them to me. This is *time sensitive*—

CHRIS: *(Really panics.)* Then make yourself throw them up—!

PAT: No!

CHRIS: Jesus, then I'm going to throw up—!

(PAT grabs CHRIS' face, firm but not mean.)

PAT: There will be no throwing up on our last date.

(CHRIS begins to cry.)

And no crying either—

CHRIS: I can't help it—

PAT: Yes, you can. Look at me. *Look at me.*

(Their faces are very close. CHRIS looks into PAT's eyes. It's hard, but CHRIS does it. PAT continues to hold her husband's face, mustering up all her energy to move through this.)

Good. Now, I will find a way to buy another bottle and do it. If not tonight, like we planned, then very soon. Do you understand this?

CHRIS: Yes—

PAT: And if I do this later, then I will be doing this alone, and I don't want to do this alone. I want the goddam love of my life by my side when I pass on. You understand this, correct?

CHRIS: I do.

PAT: And I want you to know that *I* understand this must be the worst night of your life.

CHRIS: It is—!

PAT: But it's not, Chris. You're giving me a gift by helping me avoid what *would be* the worst days of my life. Which are around the corner. I *know* you understand this. Right?

CHRIS: Yes.

PAT: Good. *(Lets go of CHRIS' face.)* Now. I've said my goodbyes to everyone else and I cannot do that again. Please, Chris. Give me this gift. I am just . . . so tired.

(A moment. From his pocket, CHRIS removes a bottle of pills—just a few left—and hands them to PAT. The hardest and most loving gesture he's ever done.)

Thank you. (*Pushing through.*) But before I do this, I have three final requests. One. I want you to tell our grandchild about me, but I don't want it to be some overblown story. I want you to be honest.

CHRIS: Of course.

PAT: Two. I want you to eat dessert every day.

CHRIS: Dessert *every* day?

PAT: Every day. That's my other regret. I wish I had eaten dessert a lot more. And three. Promise me you'll be open to the possibility of falling in love again—

CHRIS: That is not possible.

PAT: Then lie to me and say you will. I can't bear the thought of you denying yourself love because I'm dead. *Please,* Chris.

CHRIS: (*Slight hesitation.*) I promise.

(An understanding and a shared smile. Then very quickly PAT takes four pills and washes them down with her bottle of water. CHRIS is stricken but is doing his best to be there for her.)

Pat—

(PAT cuts CHRIS off with a kiss. It's their final kiss, and they both know it. They devour and allow themselves to be devoured. It's both amazing and tremendously painful to watch.)

PAT: Thank you for the best last date I could have asked for. Thank you for everything.

(A moment.)

CHRIS: Now what?

(PAT rests her head against CHRIS' chest and looks up at the stars.)

PAT: I forgot to tell you how much I love the sound of your voice. Tell me about the stars.

(It's CHRIS' turn to push through. As CHRIS points out the constellations, the light begins to fade on him. But a beam of light grows brighter on PAT.)

CHRIS: There is Perseus. Flying over Ethiopia as he holds the head of Medusa. And right there is Princess Andromeda, chained to a rock, awaiting her fate to be sacrificed to the sea monster in order to save her parents' kingdom. When Perseus sees Andromeda, he instantly falls in love and quickly tells her parents that he will rescue her, but they must allow him to marry their daughter. The king and queen agree . . .

(The light is nearly dark on CHRIS, but PAT burns bright and brilliant as the beam of light on her intensifies. PAT, now exhausted, finally closes her eyes as CHRIS continues . . .)

It's true. Perseus does use Medusa's head to turn the monster into stone, which spares Andromeda's life, and they get married. Happily ever after. But I'm not sure if it's correct to say that Perseus saved Andromeda. I actually think it's the other way around. I think . . . I *know*, that in the end, *she* is the one who saved *him*.

(The light holds on PAT for another moment. And then . . . Blackout.)

END OF PLAY

FORTY LOVE

Rich Rubin

Rich Rubin's plays have been staged throughout the United States as well as Europe, Asia, Australia, New Zealand, Mexico, and Canada. His full-length plays include *Picasso in Paris* (winner, Julie Harris Playwright Award); *Swimming Upstream* (winner, Todd McNerney Playwriting Award); *Caesar's Blood* (finalist, Oregon Book Award); *Cottonwood in the Flood* (winner, Fratti-Newman Political Play Award); *Assisted Living* (winner, Neil Simon Festival New Play Award); *Costa Rehab* (finalist, Oregon Book Award); *Left Hook* (finalist, Woodward-Newman Drama Award); *One Weekend in October* (winner, Playhouse Creatures Emerging Playwright Award); *Shakespeare's Skull* (winner, Portland Civic Theatre Guild New Play Award); *September Twelfth* (finalist, Oregon Book Award); *Marilyn/Misfits/Miller* (finalist, Julie Harris Playwright Award); and *Kafka's Joke* (finalist, Woodward International Playwriting Prize). Rich is a member of the Dramatists Guild, New Play Exchange, and Portland's Nameless Playwrights and LineStorm Playwrights. Website: richrubinplaywright.com.

SYNOPSIS

Will a couple that plays together stay together?

CHARACTERS

MAN, fortyish.
WOMAN, fortyish.

SETTING

An outdoor tennis court, somewhere in America.

TIME

Present day.

At rise: an outdoor tennis court, somewhere in present-day America. It's either daytime or nighttime under the lights. Either way is OK. A MAN and a WOMAN stand yards apart, separated by an imaginary "net." Each holds a tennis racket. These can either be real or imaginary. The MAN holds an imaginary "ball." He mimes bouncing it, then turns to face the audience.

MAN: (*To audience.*) Y'know, some people say you should never play tennis with your spouse. But I beg to differ. The way I see it: you should *only* play tennis with your spouse! I mean, why waste all that fun on anyone else—am I right? (*To the WOMAN.*) Ready, pumpkin?

WOMAN: Am I *ready?* Seriously? Listen, mister— (*Re: the "ball."*) Just smack that sucker over to Mama and see what happens!

MAN: (*To audience.*) After all, tennis is not just a sport. Not to me. Nor to my beloved just beyond the net. To us, tennis is *more* than just a sport. Isn't that true, pumpkin?

WOMAN: You bet your ass it is! *Much* more!

MAN: (*To audience.*) See what I mean? Tennis is not just a workout for your quads, a tonic for your glutes! No! Tennis is a way of life! A confluence of body and soul! A portal to the hypothalamus! A metaphor for—

WOMAN: (*Interrupting.*) Pumpkin?

MAN: Yes, love?

WOMAN: Shut up and serve!

MAN: Of course, pumpkin. I was just—

WOMAN: *Now!*

MAN: (*To audience.*) Watch closely, OK? Observe how gracefully we glide. Our ebb and flow. The yin and yang.

(*He serves the ball with a grunt.*)

Oof!

(*The WOMAN slams the ball back to him, also with a grunt.*)

WOMAN: *Oof!*

(*The ball strikes the MAN on the forehead. The MAN cries out in pain.*)

MAN: *Ow!*

WOMAN: Yay! My point! Fifteen–love!

(*She does a little celebratory dance. She's actually pretty graceful. The MAN wipes his head with his palm.*)

MAN: I think I'm bleeding.

(*The MAN shows his palm to the WOMAN.*)

WOMAN: (*Re: his non-bloody palm.*) No, you're not.

MAN: Are you sure?

WOMAN: I don't see any blood.

MAN: (*Sarcastic.*) All right. So maybe I'm not bleeding externally. Maybe just *internally.* Y'know what? I think I need a CAT scan. Or maybe an MRI. Or maybe both.

WOMAN: Quiet! Don't be such a baby! Either serve or forfeit!

MAN: (*To audience.*) Sometimes a beginner—a relative novice— evokes a benevolent smile from the gods and guess what? She scores a lucky point. Tennis *aficionados* have a special term for this phenomenon. We call it . . . "beginner's luck."

WOMAN: (*To the MAN.*) Only I'm not a beginner.

MAN: (*To audience.*) Fine. She's not a beginner. In which case, her momentary success can be explained by a vaguely similar phenomenon: "non-beginner's luck." Which is only slightly less annoying.

WOMAN: (*To the MAN.*) Are you through complaining?

MAN: Who's complaining?

WOMAN: *You*—that's who!

MAN: I'm not complaining. I'm simply providing a little context, that's all! Some helpful commentary.

WOMAN: Commentary, my ass! That's you to a "T," all right! All talk, no action!

MAN: No action, huh? Well, let's see about *that*, shall we?

WOMAN: Yes! Let's!

(*The MAN raises an index finger toward the sky. He looks up.*)

MAN: Oh, look! Up there! A hummingbird!

(*The WOMAN also looks up to the sky.*)

WOMAN: Really? Where?

(The MAN serves the ball with a quick and sneaky smash. He grunts.)

MAN: *Oof!*

(The WOMAN, caught unawares, reaches for the ball, but it skips just past her racket.)

WOMAN: Hey! I wasn't ready!

MAN: Who's complaining now, huh?

WOMAN: No fair! You cheated!

MAN: Tie score! Fifteen–fifteen!

(He does a little celebratory dance. It's half robotic, half rubbery and totally awkward.)

WOMAN: *(Re: his dance.)* What's *that* supposed to be?

MAN: *(Re: his dance.)* This? This is my victory jig!

WOMAN: A victory jig? You only have one point!

MAN: No, I don't! I have *fifteen* points!

WOMAN: That's only because in tennis, fifteen comes right after zero!

MAN: So? Don't blame me! Do I make the rules?

WOMAN: Just serve, all right? And no more stupid "hummingbird" tricks, OK?

(The MAN serves a third time, again with a grunt.)

MAN: *Oof!*

(A spirited volley follows. The MAN and the WOMAN engage in a series of surprisingly acrobatic moves, each accompanied by a grunt.)

WOMAN: *Oof!*

MAN: *Oof!*

WOMAN: *Oof!*

MAN: *Oof!*

WOMAN: *Oof!*

> *(The imaginary ball lands along the far edge of fair territory, just beyond the MAN's reach. His arm and racket fully outstretched, he swings and misses.)*

MAN: *(As he misses.) Damn!*

WOMAN: *(Exultant.)* My point! Thirty–fifteen!

> *(She does another brief celebratory dance.)*

MAN: You sure that was in?

WOMAN: Positive.

MAN: Ideally, we should ask a line judge.

WOMAN: There *is* no line judge!

MAN: Obviously. And that's why I said "ideally."

WOMAN: Do you want to argue, or do you want to serve?

MAN: Are those my only two choices?

WOMAN: Quit stalling! I'm primed for the kill!

MAN: *Kill?*

WOMAN: You heard me!

MAN: Please, pumpkin: just think what you're saying. There's more to tennis than winning, y'know.

WOMAN: I know! There's also *losing*—which is where *you* come in!

MAN: What about love?

WOMAN: Excuse me?

MAN: Love. Just think: Where would we be without it? Even worse, where would *tennis* be without it?

WOMAN: You know what? Now I *am* worried about you. Maybe you *do* need a CAT scan after all!

MAN: (*Explaining.*) No "love," no way to keep score. No way to keep score, no tennis. I mean, why hit a ball if you can't keep score? Why hit a ball without "love"?

WOMAN: Huh?

MAN: Makes perfect sense to me. What about you?

WOMAN: But "love"—

MAN: Yeah?

WOMAN: It means "nothing" in tennis!

MAN: Pumpkin!

WOMAN: What?

MAN: How could you possibly *say* that?

WOMAN: But it's true! In tennis, that's literally what "love" means! *Nada!* Zilch! Nothing!

MAN: Wow!

WOMAN: What?

MAN: I never realized you felt this way. This is like a whole other side of you.

(He starts walking away.)

WOMAN: What's going on? Are you leaving?

MAN: Well, given what you just said, why continue?

WOMAN: You mean with our marriage?

MAN: What? No! Not our marriage. This match, this game!

(Beat. The WOMAN stares at the MAN.)

WOMAN: Wait! I see what you're doing! You're leaving 'cause you're losing!

MAN: Not true.

WOMAN: Oh, yes, it is! You just can't stand to lose, can you? First, it was that dumb "hummingbird" thing—now *this*!

MAN: All right. Fine. I admit it. I *am* a little competitive—

WOMAN: A *little*?

MAN: But so are you.

WOMAN: *Me*?

MAN: Face it: we've got a problem, pumpkin. Each of us. And together, it's even worse. But I see a way out. It won't be easy, but I think we should try it.

WOMAN: What? Counseling?

MAN: Counseling? No way! *(Beat.)* Golf.

(The MAN and the WOMAN stare deeply into each other's eyes, and then the two of them stroll off together.)

END OF PLAY

GEL US

Paige Zubel

Paige Zubel (she/they) is a Philadelphia-based playwright, dramaturg, and producer. Their plays have been developed and produced by more than fifty theater companies internationally, including Berridge Conservatory (*Amos and the Stars*, Normandy, France), Normal Ave (*Dead Meat*, New York City), and What If? Productions (*A String Between Man and the World*, Charleston, South Carolina). Their plays and prose have been published by houses including Smith & Kraus, One Act Play Depot, and Hashtag Queer. She is the associate artistic director of Shakespeare in Clark Park and was the 2018–2019 recipient of the National New Play Network Producer in Residence grant through InterAct Theatre Company. They sit on the Board of The Kaleidoscapes (New York City) and the Artistic Advisory Board of Paper Doll Ensemble (Philadelphia, Pennsylvania). Writers' groups: PlayPenn's The Foundry, class of 2020; InterAct Core Playwright, class of 2021; Philadelphia Theatre Company Playwright Fellow, 2021. More of her work can be found on the New Play Exchange.

SYNOPSIS

Friends Laura and Kathy realize that running a marathon is a lot like some relationships: not worth it.

CHARACTERS

LAURA, Kathy's friend, 20s–30s.
KATHY, Laura's friend, 20s–30s.

SETTING

A street that's part of a marathon course.

TIME

Now.

Lights up on a bare stage.

LAURA, thirty-three, with a perfectly styled ponytail, black running capris, a lightweight tank top, and an unrumpled marathon number pinned to her chest, trots on stage. She looks tired, sure, but energized enough to keep pushing forward. There is a tight, manic energy pulsing in her that she is trying to suppress, or at least override, with optimism. She realizes she is alone on stage. She checks her watch. Jogging in place, she looks around for KATHY, who has still not appeared.

LAURA: Kathy? (*No response.*) Kathy, where are you? We've got to keep going.

KATHY: (*Offstage.*) I'm coming.

> (*From the same entrance as LAURA, KATHY, thirty-two, enters. KATHY's ponytail, like everything else about her, is in exponentially*

*worse shape. Her baggy T-shirt is soaked, and her painting shorts
have begun to make her chafe. Struggling, she trots up to meet
LAURA.)*

*(Both jogging in place, they turn to face the audience. LAURA is
comfortable. KATHY is in bad shape.)*

*(Still jogging, KATHY gives LAURA a look of dismay: "I can't do
this anymore.")*

(LAURA smiles it away: "You can do it.")

(KATHY gives LAURA another warning look: "No, I really can't.")

(LAURA smiles at KATHY: "You're okay.")

(KATHY starts to sink to the ground: "I'm sorry.")

(LAURA stares at KATHY: "Don't you dare, don't you dare.")

(KATHY sinks all the way to the ground.)

(LAURA stops jogging in place.)

LAURA: Get up. Get up, we've got to keep our pace up. (*No response.*)
Did you eat those orange wedges? I told you you'd crash if you didn't
eat some orange wedges. Do you need some water? I've got a little left
in my CamelBak. But don't drink it all. I think I've got some energy
gels. The blue ones kinda taste like Christmas but, like, also a little bit
expired, so maybe like Christmas in June-ish? Something like that.
Kathy? Kathy, get up.

KATHY: (*From the ground.*) Laura, I'm tired.

LAURA: It's a marathon. Of course you're tired. Come on, let's go.

KATHY: No, I mean, like, tired. Like, "done" tired.

LAURA: What? No, we've been doing great. *You've* been doing great.
Come on. Up, up, up.

KATHY: I need a break.

LAURA: You can have a break in twenty-four miles.

KATHY: I need a break now.

LAURA: We don't have time for breaks.

KATHY: *You* don't have time for breaks.

LAURA: *We*, remember. We're a team, we're in this together.

KATHY: Can we just sit for a bit? I need a breather.

LAURA: We don't have time to sit.

KATHY: Then can we just walk? Like, a really, really slow walk?

LAURA: We don't have time to walk.

KATHY: (*Waving her away.*) Then go, okay? Go. I'm fine. Leave me here with the orange wedges.

LAURA: I can't leave you here.

KATHY: I'm fine with it. Go on ahead. I'll cheer for you.

LAURA: No, I'm not leaving you here.

KATHY: You don't want to sit, you don't want to walk. I'll meet you at the finish line. You can tell me all about it.

(*Beat.*)

LAURA: You said you'd do this with me.

KATHY: I way overestimated my abilities.

LAURA: You said you didn't want to train.

KATHY: Yeah, well, that's because I hate running.

LAURA: Then why did you say you'd be my running buddy?

KATHY: Because I was trying to be nice.

LAURA: Nice?

KATHY: Yeah. Nice. First the divorce, and then David getting remarried—I figured, Laura's had a shitty year. She wants to run a marathon. I'm a good friend. I'll do it with her.

LAURA: That's nice.

KATHY: See? That's what I was going for. Nice.

LAURA: Thank you.

KATHY: You're welcome.

LAURA: But now we really need to keep moving, so I need you to get up.

KATHY: No, I can't keep up with you. I thought this was gonna be girl time. Like, we're saying we're running a marathon, but it's more like talking shit and drinking wine and stuff.

LAURA: Why would you think that?

KATHY: Because that's what we do.

LAURA: That's not all we do.

KATHY: Yes, it is. That is literally all we do.

LAURA: Sometimes we do yoga.

KATHY: No, we never do yoga. We grab the remote off your coffee table with our feet because we're too lazy to get off the couch. *Marie* does yoga. You never even mentioned yoga until David married her and Bobby said she took him to a Mommy and Me yoga class.

LAURA: I didn't know I told you that.

KATHY: Of course you did. You told me when we were talking shit and drinking wine because that is *literally* all we do. And I get it, I do, why you're all wound up about Marie—

LAURA: This has nothing to do with Marie. Why do you keep bringing her up?

KATHY: This has everything to do with Marie.

LAURA: No, it doesn't.

KATHY: Then why the hell are we running a marathon?

LAURA: Because I want to be better. Don't you want to be better?

KATHY: Better at what?

LAURA: I don't know. Life. Being healthy.

KATHY: Laura, you don't care about being healthy.

LAURA: Yes, I do. It's important.

KATHY: Sure, it's important, but you don't care. And I'm not judging you for that. I don't care, either. But this yoga-hiking-mountain-climbing-marathon-running-twenty-five-year-old shows up and marries David and starts taking your kid to Mommy and Me classes and suddenly, what, you magically become a healthy-living guru?

LAURA: I just woke up, Kathy. A few weeks ago I realized, you know what, I'm thirty-three, and I don't want to die soon, so I need to start taking care of myself. There is nothing wrong with that. There is nothing wrong with wanting to be healthy. Just because you want to pretend to be in your twenties forever doesn't mean I have to.

KATHY: People don't wake up and decide to be healthy, and then go out and run a marathon. They put fewer croutons on their salad. They get Frappuccinos without whipped cream.

LAURA: That's what you call healthy?

KATHY: That's what I call *our* healthy.

LAURA: I don't even *like* the whipped cream.

KATHY: (*Under her breath.*) Not since Marie showed up.

LAURA: What is that supposed to mean?

KATHY: It means you've *changed.*

LAURA: I haven't changed!

KATHY: Look at what you're wearing. What is that, that thing, called? A CamelBak? What *is* that? And those pants, and that exercise shirt. Running shoes? *Energy gels?* It's like you're putting on a big show for Bobby—who probably doesn't even know what the hell is going on anyway, he's *four*—like you're showing him that everything his new mommy can do, you can do better, like you're putting on this whole charade trying to one-up Marie. And I did not sign up for that.

LAURA: This is not some charade—

KATHY: (*An exasperated blurt.*) I saw her at the starting line.

LAURA: Oh.

KATHY: Yeah. Saw her and her little perky, dopey smile. And then the starting shot went off, and you just zipped outta there like someone lit a firecracker under your ass.

LAURA: I didn't know you saw her.

KATHY: So I'm right? All that healthy-eating, thirty-three-won't-be-the-death-of-me stuff was bullshit?

(*Beat.*)

LAURA: I'm sorry.

KATHY: I don't want you to be sorry.

LAURA: I should've told you.

KATHY: Yeah, you should've.

LAURA: I just needed you here. To do this with me. I didn't know if you'd come if you knew this was all about—about . . .

KATHY: Laura? Laura, are you okay?

LAURA: (*An emotional outburst.*) I HATE RUNNING.

    (*KATHY takes LAURA into her sweaty, sweaty embrace.*)

KATHY: Hey, hey, it's okay.

LAURA: I thought it would be a good idea.

KATHY: I know.

LAURA: (*Still emotionally outburst-ing.*) I follow her on Instagram, and I see her post all these pictures of kale salads and ginger-grape smoothies, and it doesn't look that hard. I thought, I can do that. I can make a ginger-grape smoothie. And then there was a picture on her feed of Bobby from the Mommy and Me, and he looked so happy. And that's my kid on her feed, *my* kid, not her kid. I just want to make him that happy on my own, you know? And then she posted this dumb picture of her marathon number she got in the mail—like, hello, you aren't an artsy photographer, you're not fooling anybody! So I signed up for this stupid marathon and bought these stupid running shoes and—I really hate running. (*Through her sobs:*) Are people staring?

KATHY: (*A lie.*) No.

LAURA: I'm sorry.

KATHY: I know.

LAURA: Do we have to finish the marathon?

KATHY: (*Gentle.*) Fuck no.

LAURA: (*Utter relief.*) Okay, good. I don't want to.

KATHY: There we go. There's Laura.

> (*KATHY stands. Her legs are jelly. When she steadies herself, she offers LAURA a helping hand and hoists her up.*)

LAURA: I really wanted to beat her.

KATHY: (*Tenderly.*) Oh, honey, that was never gonna happen.

LAURA: Do we have to tell Bobby?

KATHY: Let's drive to the finish line, take a picture. We'll just say we did it.

LAURA: We can do that?

KATHY: Of course we can do that.

LAURA: And then wine?

KATHY: Good god, yes. So much wine.

> (*LAURA, emotionally drained, and KATHY, physically exhausted, both lean on one another for support, and hobble off.*)

END OF PLAY

GERSHWIN'S LAST RIDE

Ryan Stevens

Ryan Stevens (he/they) is a playwright/director currently based in Chicago. They received an MA in theater and an MFA in playwriting from UCLA. Stevens has worked with Silver Spring Stage, MeetCute LA, The Inkwell Theater, St. Croix Falls Festival Theatre, Retrograde Reading Series, New American Theatre, Whiskey Radio Hour, Theatre Viscera, Festival D'Avignon, Broken Slate Productions, The Plagiarists Chicago, Philadelphia Dramatists Center, T. Schreiber Studio, Seoul Players, and an upcoming commission with Theatre Above the Law.

SYNOPSIS

Gershwin, a prize-winning bull, goes one-on-one with the hottest pro bull rider today, AJ Hawkins. Gershwin is renowned for his fury, already has a body count, and given the right amount of stress, he just might snap again. In ten minutes (and eight seconds), these two champions clash and leave forever changed.

CHARACTERS

TUCKY, rodeo clown. Great with kids, motor mouth.
GERSHWIN, Brangus bull. 1,842 pounds. Never been ridden for the
    full eight seconds, and damn proud of it.
AJ HAWKINS, The Next Big Thing in professional bull riding.

SETTING

A rodeo arena.

TIME

Present day.

"Rhapsody in Blue" plays as TUCKY, face brightly painted, stands juggling bowling pins center stage.

TUCKY: What do you call a bull that fell asleep at the rodeo? A bull-dozer.

What do you call a retired cowboy? De-ranged.

Why do cows wear bells? Their horns don't work.

How do you kill a rodeo clown? Go for the juggler.

   (TUCKY stops juggling.)

Y'all had enough? All right. Now my name's Tucky, Tucky the Clown. I got a boring human name, but that ain't why we're here. I'm a member of the Plucky Sisters Rodeo Clowns. There's me, there's Lucky, and there's Ducky. We always joke about our fourth sister, who's Ffff . . . fully booked at a hotel somewhere near. That joke usually kills. My sisters and I are what's called barrelmen. We clown, we joke, but when the time comes, we get down and dirty with the bulls. Ducky and Lucky are more strategic during the rides, they're the ones who secure the rider when he gets bucked off. That leaves *me* to distract the bulls until the riders are safe. And the most dangerous bull I work with, but my most fav-o-rite (*Pronounced to rhyme with "right."*) bull to witness, is none other than tonight's star.

(*Ostentatiously clears her throat—the music comes back to ring in the entrance.*)

Ladies and gentlemen, boys and girls, children of allllll ages, presenting . . . GERSHWIN!

(*GERSHWIN, a stunningly muscular and fit performer, stands flexing. He has a prominent golden septum ring and a brand on a bicep—a barbed-wire "8"—or maybe it's an infinity sign? He stands to the side, "in the chute," ready to be ridden. He throws his head and neck around every now and then, like he's swinging at flies.*)

Near on a ton of pure warrior beef. He's a right celebrity in the Professional Bull Riding circles.

GERSHWIN: Undefeated. Unridden. Unconquered.

TUCKY: Ninety-six outs and he ain't never been successfully ridden for the full eight seconds. He's Muhammad Ali with hooves, he's Samson with horns, he's a bovine Incredible Hulk.

GERSHWIN: I don't think it's impossible. It just sure ain't happenin' anytime soon. You folks aren't exactly what I'd call tenacious.

TUCKY: Another thing about Gershwin: he's got a peculiar temperament. When you ride him, he's true hellfire. But the microsecond he drops you—

GERSHWIN: The microsecond you leave my back and hit the ground, I couldn't care less about you. We're settled.

TUCKY: Once he's proved his point, it's as if he's alone in a meadow. Peaceful as one of his Wagyu beef brethren. Now, should a rider get a little too close to that eight-second mark—

GERSHWIN: Well, in that case, I might have to give them a little receipt.

TUCKY: Y'see, in all of Gershwin's no doubt illustrious career, uh, there is one touchy spot.

GERSHWIN: Go ahead. They probably know already.

TUCKY: Y'all mighta heard of one Brady Dover? 'Bout two years ago, this fella Dover, rider out in Kentucky, he matched up with Gershwin and held on for a record-setting six seconds.

GERSHWIN: He was yawping like some kind of bird. Had no business bein' up there.

TUCKY: Well, "held on" is maybe generous. He was mostly off, dragging on the side, but he still had his hand gripped on the saddle, at least until Gershwin hooked him. Damn near skewered that poor boy. He died in the hospital the next day.

GERSHWIN: I gotta be honest, I don't know what you folks get out of the bargain. Us bulls are treated well for our time—we're specimens of our kind. We get well fed, we get taken care of, and what do you folk get? Bucked. Flies get swatted, riders get bucked, Gershwin gets fed. There's gotta be something pushing these fools, but I can't figure it. I ain't against the idea of someone riding me all the way, but I don't want it to be just anyone. It ain't gonna be some upstart treatin' me like a mountain to put behind him. A bull takes umbrage at disrespect.

TUCKY: Now I know what you're thinking—*no*, I was *not* the one workin' when Brady Dover got got. That was some other clown, a real clown's clown if you ask me. Anyhoozle, on today's rodeo—

(*AJ HAWKINS enters.*)

AJ: 'Scuse me, mind if I do my own?

TUCKY: Suit yourself, shooter.

(TUCKY moves to GERSHWIN, out of the way. GERSHWIN snorts, unimpressed by this fella.)

AJ: *The* AJ Hawkins here, yeah bo! I can feel it, today's the day I'm gonna draw Gershwin. Imma draw that sonsabitch, yessir! The draw is one of my favorite parts of bein' a bull rider—you can't prepare for your enemy, you just gotta meet them on the day of. Our job is survival—any a y'all ridden a bull before, you know how it feels: like a tornado made solid and with horns! But all we gotta do is survive to the count of eight. Patience yields persistence and persistence yields victory—that's the secret to withstanding the beast! Hey! Check my representation, bo.

(AJ shows his jacket, covered in sponsorship patches. GERSHWIN, still watching, tilts his head, confused.)

All these bigwig sponsors ain't got no idea about bull ridin', ain't never hauled hay, ain't never worn boots wasn't designer, all they know is *I* am a *name*. Let me tell ya folks, I wake up smilin' damn near every morning. Does it make me mad these carpetbaggers are using me to feel like their brand of whatever is worth something? *Hell* no! That's the modern cowboy, y'all hear? We been ran out of physical frontier— we only got the frontier of the mind.

(AJ closes his eyes, breathes deep, and stretches his arms out.)

And AJ Hawkins is gonna storm that frontier as long and as hard as he can.

(Lights shift, and we hear the distorted voice of an announcer. AJ stands behind GERSHWIN, ready to mount. TUCKY stands to the side, speaking to the audience.)

TUCKY: And here we are, folks. The main event. The moment of truth. AJ and Gershwin.

AJ's about to mount, he won't quit muggin' to the cameras. He's really peacocking it. But then he turns to one part of the audience, points to someone, and blows a kiss. And it ain't any rockstar kiss or nothin', it's simple. Sincere.

I never did find out who it was to.

AJ: I told all my family to watch this. I told them this was gonna be a big day for me, I could feel it. I got my sweetheart here, blow a kiss in the general area. I know it'll find its target. And then I turn my thoughts to glory.

GERSHWIN: You people really like to act like surviving is special. It's not special, everyone who's alive is doing it.

TUCKY: Y'all ready?

> *(GERSHWIN and AJ both nod to her, AJ ready to mount. TUCKY gives a "go" sign to someone offstage.)*

The gate opens. The clock starts ticking. The air heats up. They start the ride.

> *(AJ "mounts" GERSHWIN—it more resembles Greco-Roman wrestling. During the following, they stylize the ride.)*

AJ: This is my day, y'all. Yee-yee!

TUCKY: Gershwin starts out spinnin' like a top—he likes to spin most times, but usually he'll take a second or two to just straight-up buck. But he's in a rush today. Hawkins holds on.

TUCKY, AJ, and GERSHWIN: One second.

AJ: He's whippin' me like them hurricane winds, I tell you what, but I trained for this. I felt this comin'. I stay.

TUCKY, AJ, and GERSHWIN: Two seconds.

GERSHWIN: Buck my back legs and jerk my head back, try to crack AJ in the face—

AJ: Ooh, you clever, huh, boy?

TUCKY: Holy shit, that's weird. Another bull did that to Hawkins about a year ago—

AJ: You bulls been gossipin'? Or are you just a fan of my work, Gershwin?

TUCKY, AJ, and GERSHWIN: Three seconds.

TUCKY: AJ ain't smilin' anymore. He's laser-focused, his mouth is doing little spasms as he puts all his brainpower into holdin' on. My sisters and I are ready for this to go sideways at any time.

GERSHWIN: Fall! Damn your futile bones, fall!

TUCKY, AJ, and GERSHWIN: Four seconds.

AJ: Blood in my mouth tastes like sweet bourbon.

TUCKY: Gershwin does a straight-lookin' vertical jump, and AJ's body bounces like a stack of Legos thrown on the floor. Swear I hear somethin' in his leg snap.

AJ: Both legs. Sometimes it be like that.

TUCKY: But he still holds on. The audience is losing it. They're hooping and hollering, feels like WrestleMania in here.

TUCKY, AJ, and GERSHWIN: Five seconds.

GERSHWIN: I want him off. He feels like a tick. He is draining me.

AJ: Come on, Gershwin, push me! This is history, new frontier, baybay!

GERSHWIN: Make a dash for the pen's walls, scrape him off. Like shit off a boot.

TUCKY: Every juke and jump makes the crowd gasp like banshees.

TUCKY, AJ, and GERSHWIN: Six seconds.

TUCKY: He's still here.

TUCKY, AJ, and GERSHWIN: *Six seconds.*

AJ: Yee-yee!

GERSHWIN: Will you stop that!

TUCKY: By still breathing right here, Hawkins has already made history.

AJ: Pio-fuckin-neering!

TUCKY: He could let go now and still end the day a superhero. But he doesn't.

GERSHWIN: Maybe I'd be disappointed if he did let go. Maybe this is something special. But I won't make it easy.

AJ: I'm doing it I'm doing it I'm doing it—

TUCKY and AJ: Seven seconds!

AJ: Manifest Goddamn Destiny!

TUCKY: Seven. The crowd is rabid! My team and I feel like we're watchin' a new pope get born . . .

GERSHWIN: Each tick of the clock electrifies me like the cattle prod—

AJ: I will forge this path! Y'all're my witnesses!

TUCKY: It's happening! It's all happening! Here it is! The clock ticks it up!

Eight sec—

(GERSHWIN finally bucks AJ off.)

GERSHWIN: Seven-point-eight-eight.

TUCKY: Seven-point-eight-eight.

AJ: Seven-point-eight-eight.

TUCKY: My girls and I are runnin' I know we're movin', we got the muscle memory even if in my mind this moment is frozen—

Gershwin stares at AJ. AJ stares at Gershwin. I run between them. I do my job. *I am there.* I stare at Gershwin, wavin' and callin', but . . .

GERSHWIN: I don't see her. I don't see anything. Nothing but red.

AJ: I don't see her either. Only Gershwin. I see him. I fall to my knees. Not from pain, not from my splinters of bone. I fall to my knees in perfect understanding.

TUCKY: And then, it happens—

(GERSHWIN vaults over TUCKY and dashes at AJ and punches him square on the temple. AJ falls over.)

He was too fast to stop—and he wasn't distracted at all. He stomped AJ right on the melon. AJ was killed straight away. Didn't feel nothin', they say. Gershwin did it, then looked back—and kinda. Froze. Like he was surprised. And then he went back down the chute, no guiding needed. Horns pointed down low.

GERSHWIN: Stupid. Embarrassing. Who did this? Was this me? I wasn't in my head. Stupid.

(GERSHWIN crosses to a corner upstage, sullen. TUCKY pulls AJ's body off to the side. She then wipes off her clown makeup during the following.)

TUCKY: After Gershwin's second kill, his owner made a statement saying the old bull would be retired. He'd live the rest of his days on his owner's ranch, unbothered and undefeated and unchallenged, with two bloody asterisks hanging over his legacy.

Gershwin's owner leaves for the night, he's got officials to talk to, doctors, lawyers . . . he doesn't take Gershwin away immediately. I can't bear to leave either. Once I walk out, that's that. It's no longer happening, just happened. The frozen past tense.

I feel like I owe y'all an apology. I might seem like a liar, but I'm not. I'm just wrong. Guess now I'm the clown's clown.

(GERSHWIN takes a step toward her.)

GERSHWIN: Tucky.

TUCKY: Easy there, killer. That was in you always, huh? Dover and now Hawkins. Shoulda known.

GERSHWIN: I lost my head. I admit it.

TUCKY: Yeah, well, keep your distance before I lose mine.

What do you call the feeling where you've heard the same line of bull before? Deja-moo.

GERSHWIN: Resent me all you want. I won't push back on it.

TUCKY: What you did has weight to it, Gershwin!

GERSHWIN: I don't pretend it doesn't.

(TUCKY steps toward GERSHWIN.)

TUCKY: No one knows you better'n me, and turns out what I know ain't worth a hill of beans.

GERSHWIN: I can't be done yet. Give me my dignity, Tucky. You *do* know me, you're the only one who does.

TUCKY: Oh yeah?

(TUCKY slowly approaches GERSHWIN, one hand outstretched, careful. GERSHWIN bows his head slightly and takes her hand.)

Oh, would you look at that. Looks like I've drawn Gershwin. Let's see if I know you.

(She rides him. Not like a wrestling contest now, but more synchronous—at times it seems like GERSHWIN is carrying her. A piece similar to "Mad Rush" by Philip Glass plays as GERSHWIN lets TUCKY ride him for a full eight seconds, in real time.)

One.

Two.

Three.

Four.

Five.

Six.

Seven . . .

(TUCKY is now holding GERSHWIN, gently.)

GERSHWIN: Eight.

Now go and tell them. Tell them I'm just a bull after all. I'm an honest bull.

TUCKY: It's okay now, fella. You made it. The ride's over.

(Lights down.)

END OF PLAY

HAROLD'S ISLAND

Jackie Martin

Jackie Martin is a teacher and playwright from Norwood, Massachusetts. Her plays include *Hallmark Doesn't Make Cards for Us*, *Corrections*, *No Right Time*, *We're Alright*, *Impressions*, and *Abigail, For Now*. Jackie's work has been produced by Shadblow Theatre, Left Edge Theatre, Playwrights' Round Table, Open Theatre Project, the Warner Theatre, Firehouse Center for the Arts, SUNY Brockport, Southern Oregon University, SUNY Plattsburgh, and others. Awards include the Peter Honegger Prize for Best Short Play and the Peter Honegger Prize for Best One-Act. Jackie's work has been published by YouthPLAYS and Smith & Kraus. She is a member of the Lochstead Writers, Playwrights' Platform, and the Dramatists Guild of America. Jackie's plays can be found on the New Play Exchange.

SYNOPSIS

Daniel, desperate and afraid, has just washed up on an island in the middle of the ocean. He's relieved to meet Harold, an inhabitant of the island. Unfortunately, he's really getting in the way of Harold's peace and quiet.

CHARACTERS

DANIEL, a man in his 30s or 40s. Afraid, lost, looking worse for the
wear. Any race/ethnicity.

HAROLD, a man in his 50s or 60s. Has been living in peace by himself
on the island for about a year. Any race/ethnicity.

SETTING

A small, mostly deserted island in the middle of the Pacific Ocean.

TIME

Summer, 2019. Daytime.

NOTE

If the director wishes, the year referenced in the play may be adjusted to
reflect that the story is taking place in the same year as the production.

A deserted island in the middle of the sea. Some coconuts may litter the
stage, but that's about it. DANIEL enters, crawling. He stops and lies on
his back, breathing heavily, moaning in exhaustion and pain. After a
moment, he pulls himself to a sitting position. He has a small, beat-up
bag. He pulls out a bottle of water, which is gone after he takes a swig.

DANIEL: Ah, shit. (*He looks around.*) Where am I? Oh, God.

> (*DANIEL lies back and puts his hands over his face. He turns onto his*
> *stomach and lies still, resting. HAROLD enters, carrying a few fish on*
> *a line and humming softly. DANIEL does not hear him. HAROLD*
> *suddenly sees DANIEL and screams. DANIEL screams back.*)

HAROLD: Holy— Who the hell are you?

DANIEL: Oh my God! Are you real? Are you one of those things—are you a mirage? Am I losing it? Jesus in heaven, I've lost it, haven't I?

HAROLD: Yeah. No! I mean, no, you haven't—I mean, I'm real.

DANIEL: Oh, thank you, God. Please, is there a town nearby—do you have a phone? I need to call someone, I need to call my wife—

HAROLD: Who are you? Are you alone?

DANIEL: Please, you have to help me. Bring me to wherever you came from—

HAROLD: I'm from Oregon.

DANIEL: Please—what?

HAROLD: How did you get here?

DANIEL: I'm in Oregon? I thought this was an island. I don't understand—

HAROLD: (*Slowly.*) How—did—you—get—here?

DANIEL: A raft. I got here in a raft. Please, can you—is that fish?

HAROLD: What?

(*He quickly puts the fish behind his back.*)

No.

DANIEL: You have fish!

HAROLD: No, I don't.

DANIEL: Please, I haven't eaten in two days.

HAROLD: You know what, I take back what I said. I'm a mirage.

DANIEL: What? No—

HAROLD: Yup, so uh, go ahead back to sleep, and when you wake up, I'll be gone and you'll realize I was a figment of your imagination.

DANIEL: Stop! Don't go! I don't know—where am I? Please.

(HAROLD stops reluctantly.)

I've been at sea for days. Where are we?

HAROLD: All right. The truth is—I don't know exactly where we are. It *is* an island. And there's no town, nothing. There's . . . no one else here.

DANIEL: No one?

HAROLD: Sorry.

DANIEL: How long have you been here?

HAROLD: Uh . . . what year is it?

DANIEL: Holy shit.

HAROLD: Landed here, let's see—summer of 2018.

DANIEL: That was last year.

HAROLD: Huh. Wow. Last year? Well, you know. Time flies and all that. So, listen, you're looking pretty okay over there. Little burned maybe, but I don't see any blood, no broken bones, so if it's all the same to you—

DANIEL: I was out with my buddy Gary, we were fishing. We were way out in the ocean and after a few hours the engine started smoking. We'd been drinking all day on the boat—so stupid. We usually take our kids fishing, but this time it was only me and him and we thought, we'll have a few beers, like old times—everything stopped, the engine died—we tried to call for help but we couldn't get a signal—

HAROLD: Look, I really don't think—

DANIEL: Gary started panicking, and I tried to calm him down and he hit me.

(A beat as DANIEL remembers.)

He started hitting me and pushing me, and I thought I was going to go over the side so I—I was only trying to stop him. I punched him. I punched—he fell over and into the water. Oh, God. I didn't mean to. I didn't mean to hit him so hard. I was panicked and full of adrenaline— He fell into the water, and I lost track of him so fast. I dove in, and I looked for him. I'm not a great swimmer. I could barely stay above water, and we were so far out. I didn't know what was out there. Sharks, or . . .

(A beat. DANIEL is lost in the memory.)

I tried. The water was dark. I pulled myself back up onto the boat, but the engine was smoking. I gathered up as much as I could, all the water on board, some food, just in case—and then I waited. I kept searching for Gary. I kept trying to call the Coast Guard, my wife, anyone. Oh, God. My wife . . . I'm never going to see my wife again, am I?

(He looks to HAROLD, who looks away.)

The smoke turned to fire. I didn't know what to do—I couldn't stay there any longer, it had already been hours and Gary, he was gone—and the boat was still smoking . . . and drifting. . . . There was a small raft in the boat, so I took what I could fit and . . . You've really been here a year?

HAROLD: Just me and the sound of the waves. Till today.

DANIEL: Are you going to cook those?

HAROLD: Listen, man—

DANIEL: Daniel.

HAROLD: I've been on my own here a long time. I think it would be best if, you know—if you found, maybe, another place to settle in? If you walk about two miles that way, there's a nice spot of beach. You can get yourself set up there.

DANIEL: You can't be serious.

HAROLD: I'll help you out. I can get you set up with a shelter, show you how to make a fire. I'll give you one of the fish for tonight, and tomorrow you can start getting your own food. Okay?

DANIEL: No! Not okay!

HAROLD: Listen, this is hard for you. I get it. It's hard for me, too. You're the first person I've seen in . . . well, it feels like forever.

DANIEL: But you want to get rid of me? It makes no sense. None of this makes sense.

HAROLD: I've kind of gotten used to being alone out here. Don't get me wrong, now. I wouldn't turn away a rescue. But since you're not here to rescue me, I think it'd be better if . . . you know . . . you stay on that side of the island, and I'll stay on my side.

DANIEL: Please . . . I'll be quiet. I won't bother you.

HAROLD: I've known you for about four minutes, and you've already confessed to a murder.

DANIEL: I did? Oh, Christ. I did. Gary.

HAROLD: No, I get it—you didn't mean to, you were protecting yourself, blah blah blah—but, Dan—can I call you Dan?

DANIEL: Okay.

HAROLD: Dan, that's not really a *four-minutes-in* kind of conversation, you know? And that's probably only the beginning. You seem like a guy who shares. I'm not much into sharing.

DANIEL: Look, I . . . I don't know your name.

HAROLD: Yeah, not much into sharing.

DANIEL: You can't abandon me! Please! I don't know how to get food, or where to find fresh water—where have you been getting water?

HAROLD: Mostly I drink coconut milk . . . collect water when it rains. It actually rains fairly often, though not all day or anything. Spurts here and there throughout the day. Buddy, I know you're new here, but like I said, I can show you—

DANIEL: I'm new here? I'm *new* here?

HAROLD: Okay, relax. You've been out in the sun, you haven't eaten, you need to calm down. It's not good for you to get all worked up.

DANIEL: How exactly should I calm down? How the hell am I going to get off this island? Tell me. Has anyone even come close to rescuing you? Have you ever seen a barge? A helicopter, anything?

   (HAROLD is uncomfortable. He doesn't respond.)

And now you want to throw me to the wolves.

HAROLD: There has been no evidence of wolves on this island.

DANIEL: You know what I mean!

   (Beat.)

Oh my God. I'm going to die here. And I deserve it. I killed Gary.

HAROLD: You don't know that for sure.

DANIEL: This is my punishment.

HAROLD: And if Gary's dead, you know, it's not totally your fault. You said it yourself, he attacked you.

   (DANIEL lies back again and puts his arms across his face.)

DANIEL: It's over. It's all over.

(HAROLD begins to walk away while DANIEL is not looking, but stops. He looks back at DANIEL. We see him consider his options before making a decision. He's not exactly happy about the decision he's making, but he makes it. He sits down next to DANIEL on the sand.)

HAROLD: I was flying alone.

DANIEL: What?

HAROLD: I was flying alone. You're not supposed to do that. The plane went down.

DANIEL: You're a pilot.

HAROLD: I sell insurance. Sold. But I have my pilot's license, and I bought this little plane. It wasn't in the best shape, but, you know. It seemed good enough. Dan, a piece of advice. Don't buy a plane that's only "good enough." Airplanes are something to invest in.

DANIEL: How have you done it? Survived so long?

HAROLD: I guess I'm good at it. I mean, I went camping with my family growing up, and I've always been into fishing. I've hunted a couple of times, in my younger years. But, man, when I first landed here, I was just like you. Panicked, despondent. I wondered what I had done wrong in my life to get this level of shit dumped on my head, you know? I'm not a bad guy. I ran an honest business, helped people when I could. I gave to charities. I was good to my ex. I lived a nice, boring life.

I got my pilot's license to, you know, get a little adventure in my life. I'd only taken the plane out a few times before I crashed. I got my adventure, I guess. Turns out, my very basic survival skills have served me pretty well. I figured I'd be a goner, but after a couple of weeks, I gained some confidence. Getting my own food, fending for myself—it feels good. It feels natural, like this is the way it was always supposed to be. And I started enjoying the quiet. Truthfully, even if we were rescued tomorrow, I couldn't go back to my old life. Not the way I was living it before.

DANIEL: Well, you don't have to worry about that. We're not getting rescued. That much is clear.

HAROLD: You don't know that.

DANIEL: You've been here for a year.

HAROLD: But that's me. Different situation. I went out flying one Friday by myself. Didn't tell anyone, didn't have any plans for the whole weekend. No one would have been looking for me until—I don't even know. Maybe until clients called my boss to complain that I was ignoring them? I've always been a loner. I never had a Gary, you know? No kids, no siblings. My parents are dead. I even got a job where I could work out of my house. I was so caught up in my own little world—I didn't really try to make friends in my adult life. I only had acquaintances. But you—you've got a wife, a family. Did people know where you and Gary were going?

DANIEL: Yes. Yes, we always went to the same general area. Our families will know where to go.

HAROLD: So, they'll find the boat, if they haven't already. They'll see that the raft is gone. They'll come looking for you.

DANIEL: You think?

HAROLD: Sure.

(*Both men look out at the horizon.*)

DANIEL: Tomorrow. Tomorrow, I'll get out of your way. But I can't walk that far right now. I can't . . . I can't be by myself again. Not yet.

HAROLD: Look, you seem like a nice guy—

DANIEL: (*Explosive.*) What is your problem? I get that you've been out here on your own, I get that you've somehow gotten used to being stranded all alone on an island, however twisted and confusing that is. But I'm not exactly there yet. And I'm not one of your clients, man. I'm not some ghost from your past life. You think you're the only one ever hated his job? You think you're special because you felt like you were missing out on something? Jesus, that's insulting.

(HAROLD appears as if he's going to interject.)

No, no, I get it. You're a "loner." Big man. Big man's a loner. Likes to be alone. Keep telling yourself that. But is it at all possible you didn't have friends because you're an asshole?

(Pause.)

I'm a human being, man. I'm not asking you to lug me around on your back. Just be a person. Have some humanity. I'm tired, and my throat feels like it's on fire, and I'm somehow stuck on an island with the most selfish prick who ever walked the earth.

HAROLD: I mean . . . that feels harsh.

DANIEL: Forget it.

(He begins to get emotional.)

I want to go home . . . I don't want to die out here. I know I need to eat, but I don't really feel hungry, and I think that's a bad sign. That's a bad sign, right?

HAROLD: *(After a moment.)* You know what? Okay. Stay. We'll see how things go for a couple of days and decide from there. Yeah?

DANIEL: Yeah. Yes. Thank you.

HAROLD: You know how to start a fire?

DANIEL: Only what I've seen in movies. But I know how to clean a fish.

HAROLD: All right. You clean, I'll cook.

DANIEL: Thank you.

HAROLD: Here you go.

(HAROLD hands DANIEL the fish and a knife or sharp tool out of his pocket.)

DANIEL: Thank you, uh—

HAROLD: Harold.

DANIEL: Harold. Can I call you Hank?

HAROLD: No.

(Lights out.)

END OF PLAY

HOW YOU GET BURNED

Brianna Barrett

Brianna Barrett is a writer and monologist from Portland, Oregon. Her theatrical work has been developed with LineStorm Playwrights, Theater Masters, Theatre 33, HART Theatre, Bag&Baggage Productions, and UCLA. Her full-length plays *36 Perfectly Appropriate Mealtime Conversations* and *Florence Fane in San Francisco* were Eugene O'Neill National Playwrights Conference semifinalists, and she was named "Portland's Best Spoken Word/Storyteller" in *Willamette Week*'s Best of Portland awards in 2016 and 2017. Her solo show *True Love and Other Noncommunicable Diseases* was recently adapted as a five-part miniseries for the KBNB podcast. Website: briannabarrett.com.

SYNOPSIS

A fraud investigator is caught by the person he's investigating. She has some questions.

CHARACTERS

GABE, 40s–50s, male, has been in his car for way too many hours.
AUBREY, 30s–40s, female, wears comfortable pants.

SETTING

A neighborhood street.

TIME

Early evening (enough so that car headlights might look cool).

A car is parked along the curb of a neighborhood street, headlights on, casting GABE in noirish light. He smokes a cigarette.

GABE: It's not hard to become a private investigator. You take a training course, pay a licensing fee, and you're in. You don't have to be especially smart or have work experience. Perfect job for a person like me. Plus, you get to catch bad guys.

(GABE gets into the car, the window down.)

Now, I'd never have my lights on like this—that was for dramatic effect. It's not a glamorous job. I spend fifty hours a week in my car doing *nothing* ninety percent of the time, waiting for something to happen. Can't turn the car on, so it's either balls hot or freezing cold. Either way, we're all definitely pissing in a Gatorade bottle several times a day.

(AUBREY comes out of the front door.)

I'd been watching Aubrey for a week. And I messed up. I don't usually smoke, but I was smoking. My hand hanging outta my window like so. Very unprofessional. Rookie move on my part. I shoulda known better.

AUBREY: HEY!

(AUBREY approaches. GABE tries to roll up the window but isn't fast enough.)

What are you doing here?

GABE: Uuhh. I'm lost. Looking up directions.

AUBREY: Bullshit, I've seen you parked out here for days.

GABE: I'm . . . trying to work up the courage to talk to my long-lost father.

> *(AUBREY stares at him, unmoved.)*

Ran out on me and Moms when I was three. Just have faint memories of him, ya know? He had this . . . mustache. (*Notices AUBREY's skepticism.*) He might not anymore! I don't know. It's been thirty . . . (*He squints, counting.*) . . . ish . . . years. Thirty—thirty, almost forty years. So I don't remember his face. Only that mustache. It's all I know of him. And his address, I guess. Maybe.

AUBREY: . . . I'm calling the cops.

GABE: I don't know why I said mustache.

AUBREY: You have a camera.

GABE: I'm leaving now. Sorry to bother you.

> *(He rolls up the window. AUBREY stands in front of his car. GABE comes back out.)*

You think I'm a creep, but you're throwing yourself in front of my car? What's the game plan here?

AUBREY: You're not gonna run me over. You're from the insurance company, aren't you?

> *(GABE looks away.)*

Yes, I'm still sick. Will be for my whole life. Sorry that's expensive and inconvenient for a multimillion-dollar company. Not exactly a dream scenario for me either.

GABE: I'm just doing my job. I don't mean that in a weird evil minion "just my job" kind of way. I mean . . . if you have a legitimate claim, you'll be fine. I want you to be fine! If you should be! You probably should be. I'm not really supposed to have an opinion.

AUBREY: You're not supposed to have an opinion.

GABE: Not in a heartless way. Just in an objective, doin' the best job possible way. If you're really sick—awesome. Or, not *awesome*, but, you know, good for keeping your disability payments.

AUBREY: Do I look sick to you?

GABE: I don't know. I just collect the information.

AUBREY: You just secretly film me without talking to me, send that to someone else who doesn't talk to me or see me, and they decide if I'm still disabled.

GABE: I've caught a lot of pretty flagrant fraudsters in my day, you'd be surprised. Had a subject one time who was s'posed to be bedridden with some back injury—come to find he's working as a whitewater rafting instructor. Making *bank*! Collecting money from unemployment *and* disability while he's out there splashing around in the river having a grand ol' time. He thought no one would figure it out.

AUBREY: You sound proud of yourself.

GABE: Everyone needs to take pride in what they do.

AUBREY: I'm told I'll be in treatment the rest of my life. I'm young— I'm going to cost my insurance company a lot of money over the years, and I'm hoping I get a *lot* of years. They'd love to wiggle out of it. But I have a good lawyer. You know why? Because I was one. Which means I also know
that *you* know
that now that *I* know you're following me,

this no longer counts as an investigation. It counts as harassment. So I better not see you out here again.

GABE: Loud and clear. Can't promise they won't try to send someone else though.

(GABE motions like he'll get back into his car. AUBREY hesitates.)

AUBREY: Why did you take this job? Was it always your dream?

GABE: Kinda fell into it.

AUBREY: You're not very good. I've seen you out here with your window down, all hours of the day, smoking your cigarette—you're not stealthy! Are you even trying?

GABE: I don't usually smoke. It's been kind of a shit week.

AUBREY: You ever have someone tell you it might be your last?

GABE: Not directly.

AUBREY: Do you have kids?

GABE: Why are you asking?

AUBREY: I don't know. I want to know that you're human.

GABE: Pinch me.

AUBREY: I didn't say I want to know if you're *dreaming*. I want to know that the guy who comes to my house trying to catch me *not seeming sick enough* is . . . a person with feelings who cares about things.

GABE: In your experience, are a lot of people NOT real people? Shit, what about that guy over there?

(GABE points out a guy in the distance walking his dog.)

Bro's always picking up his dog's poop but leaving the bag on the sidewalk, so—I don't know, alien maybe? Do you think?

AUBREY: He's the worst. He lives, like, eight blocks away, but I swear his dog poops *exclusively* on this street. I'd pick it up, but I'd hate to be caught overextending myself.

GABE: . . . I have a daughter.

(GABE holds up his phone, showing her the photo he uses as his background image.)

AUBREY: She's cute. From what I can tell. There's a lot of apps in the way. I've never completely understood making someone's face the background image on your phone, covering it up with all the other stuff we do. Almost seems like a metaphor . . . an attempt to prioritize someone, but there's always something in the way.

GABE: Uhh . . . K.

AUBREY: Is there always something in the way?

GABE: You're a weird lady.

AUBREY: Maybe it's the cancer.

GABE: Really?

AUBREY: I don't need a reason to want to know who you are—you've been spying on me. Why'd you make up a story about having a long-lost father?

GABE: I guess that's what was at the top of my mind. I don't have a long-lost father . . . I don't want to be one either.

AUBREY: You spend time with her?

GABE: Weekends.

AUBREY: Is that hard?

GABE: Yeah.

AUBREY: What made you start smoking again?

GABE: You are the nosiest person I ever met.

AUBREY: I get that a lot, but from a *surveillance professional*?!

GABE: Hey, I didn't get into this line of work because I like being up in other people's business. I'm a loner. Really. I stay out of people's personal lives.

AUBREY: You keep a close eye on the people you *don't* know and not on the people you *do*.

GABE: Look, I don't want this to blow back and ruin my life somehow—I shouldn't be telling you any of this stuff, so . . .

  (GABE makes moves to get back into his car.)

AUBREY: What do you know about me?

GABE: I really can't tell you.

AUBREY: Do you know what I wear when I take out the trash? The nicknames I call my husband? What time he goes to work?

GABE: . . . I told you, I have a kid.

AUBREY: What would you do if you could do anything?

GABE: I don't know. "Nothing," I guess.

AUBREY: Do you think that's what I do? I can't have kids. I can't work—

GABE: —No one is making you!

AUBREY: Last time they sent someone looking for evidence of fraud, they got a photo of me grabbing something from the driver's side of my mom's car. Tried to use it as proof that I've been driving, which is one of my restrictions. I could have lost everything.

GABE: I'm sorry that happened.

AUBREY: Because I get seizures. That's why I don't drive. Back when I was younger, my car was my sanctuary. Felt like a new life was always at my fingertips. God, I miss driving. Now I can't. But someone wanted to make it seem like I do.

GABE: If it makes any difference, I'm not the guy who took that photo.

AUBREY: You sure you're not gonna be that guy in the next case you work?

GABE: I'm not out here trying to screw the little guy. I *am* the little guy. You want to know why I've been smoking? My ex wants to move out of state, so . . . there's custody stuff. I've been anxious, got sloppy on the job. And I *need* this job. Okay? It isn't the life I picked for myself, but it's the one I got.

AUBREY: I didn't pick any of this. I had a career, I was ambitious, I could argue anyone in or out of anything. Now I have—you, standing here waiting to see if I'm lying about not being able to do my old job. A job I loved, by the way. It kills me that I can't do it, and then I have to spend all this time justifying why I can't!

GABE: I don't know who was on your case before, but I only take down bad guys.

AUBREY: Do you always go in hoping they're bad guys?

GABE: It feels good to catch someone red-handed, someone who deserves to be caught. Of course.

AUBREY: Were you hoping I was a bad guy?

GABE: . . .

AUBREY: What does that make you?

GABE: Maybe *hope* is the wrong word.

AUBREY: Maybe it's the wrong hope.

GABE: I'm just doing what I gotta do.

AUBREY: Right. You're just doing what you gotta do.
You watch my family from your car.
You've seen me in my slippers.
Carrying in the groceries. How many I can carry.
And how many steps I take before I have to stop and catch my breath.
What days I'm alone.

> *(GABE's headlights turn on, AUBREY freezes in time like a memory in that noirish light. GABE looks back at the audience, reclaiming some part of himself that still wants to be our narrator.)*

GABE: I didn't see Aubrey again after that. Got my act together, stopped smoking on the job. Never got burned by any other subjects of any other investigations. Went back to being professionally unnoticeable. Private.
She stayed in my head, though.

AUBREY: "What do you know about me?"

GABE: A simple question but . . . what do we ever know about someone else?

AUBREY: "I can't have kids."

GABE: I didn't ask how she felt.

AUBREY: "My car was my sanctuary. Felt like a new life was always at my fingertips."

GABE: I didn't ask why she needed to believe she could pick up and start life somewhere else. I didn't tell her I feel that way too. Maybe she knew. She's the only person I've ever met—in my *life*—who asked me questions about myself. And I don't know why.
I do know how much weight she could carry though.

How many steps she could take.
I thought I did anyway.

> *(The headlights go out, leaving AUBREY in darkness. GABE gets into the car.)*

END OF PLAY

I CAN FLY

Gary Sironen

Gary Sironen is a playwright, composer, lyricist, arranger, director, and musician. He has written or collaborated on several short plays, full-length plays, and musicals. He self-produced a full-length musical, *Reformation*. *I Can Fly* was performed as a video play for the Columbus Black Theatre Festival in 2020, premiered live in 2021 at The Sauk's "Sauk Shorts" in Jonesville, Michigan, and was selected for production at the Itinerant Theatre, Lake Charles, Louisiana. Gary has been director and/or music director for school, church, and community theater musicals; he has composed numerous worship songs and choral anthems, performed with professional bands, and has worked as a public school band and choir director and as a church music director. Gary is a member of the Dramatists Guild of America and the Grand Rapids Federation of Musicians, Local 56 of the American Federation of Musicians. Website: garysironen.com.

SYNOPSIS

In this monologue, a student named Teri realizes they are "different" only when their mother begins to cover it up and a friend advises Teri to be careful in sharing it. Teri learns that others have secrets as well, but secrets may become harmful and dangerous.

CHARACTERS

TERI is a junior high or early high school student, nongender-specific.

SETTING

Outdoors, alone, and quiet.

TIME

A quiet day.

Stage is bare, dark except for light center. TERI enters and faces the audience.

TERI: (*Tentative.*) My name is Teri. I can fly.

   (*Pauses for a few moments, trying to decide what to say next.*)

It isn't something I tell many people about. It's a secret.

   (*Beat.*)

I don't remember when I first knew I could fly. I remember I could walk and run; then one day I could jump. And then one day I jumped a little farther, and a little farther, and then one day when I jumped . . . I just kept going.

That first time I kept going was pretty scary, 'cause I didn't know how to stop. I gradually started slowing down and getting closer to the ground. I tripped when my foot hit the ground, and I scraped my knee. Then I did it a few more times and got better at landing.

The first person I told was my mom, but not right away. Mom and Dad used to get so upset because I would jump up into a tree in our backyard, but I was too afraid to jump back down. It looked too far. So, my dad would have to get a ladder and climb up and get me and make me stay in my room until I promised to never do it again. But I did do it again.

They never saw how I got up there, and they never asked; they assumed I climbed up, I guess. Dad even cut off some lower branches, but I still got up there. One day while I was in my sad place in my room—that was a corner I sat in when they were mad at me—Mom came in to talk with me. She acted kind of funny, like she didn't know what to say. She was quiet for a while before she started to talk.

She asked me, "Teri, do you climb up in that tree?" Not "how do you get up in the tree" or "why do you go up in that tree." She just said, "Do you climb?" I didn't think about that until later. Anyway, I said, "No." I was waiting for the next question, but there wasn't one. She said, "Don't go up in that tree again. It's dangerous; you could fall out and get seriously hurt or die. Do you understand?" I said, "Yes." And that was all.

I didn't think much about it then because I assumed everyone could do it. I had cousins who would come to visit, and we would race or chase each other around, but they never jumped and kept going, so I didn't either. I didn't think about why; it was like, we never danced when we were running, and we never jumped, so . . .

Another day when I was in my sad spot for jumping, Mom came into my room again and asked, "How do you get up in that tree?"

I said, "I jump and keep going 'til I get to where I want."

She didn't ask me what I meant. She never did. She just said, "I don't want you jumping like that anymore. It isn't safe. Do you understand?"

I said, "Yes, Mom." I didn't understand. And I didn't stop.

When I started school, us kids would play and run around in the schoolyard, and nobody jumped like me, so I didn't, either. But one day, my friend Johnny and I were playing with a Frisbee, and it got stuck in a tree branch above our heads where we couldn't reach. So, I jumped up and got it. No one else was around or looking, I guess, but Johnny's eyes got really big, and he said, "How did you do that?"

I said, "I jumped."

He looked at me for a minute, then we went back to playing.

Another time, Johnny and I were playing on the swing set, just the two of us after school with no one else around. I got tired, so I got off my swing. Johnny kept swinging, and he was swinging real high and suddenly flew right out of the swing. He was thrown straight out at first, but then he started falling, so I jumped up and put my arms around him. And then we came back down and landed on our feet. (*Chuckles.*) He looked pretty scared; he tilted his head and looked at me and said, "Teri, can you fly?"

I said, "Fly?"

Johnny said, "Yeah. You flew up and caught me and brought us both down safe. How did you do that?"

I said, "I can't fly, I jumped. Anybody can do that."

And he said, "No. Nobody can do what you just did. You can fly."

The next day, Johnny told a couple of other kids that I could fly. They laughed and started teasing him. Then, they came over to me and asked me if I could fly. I didn't know what to say. I was confused because I never thought of it as flying. They were making fun of Johnny, and I felt bad for him, but I didn't want them making fun of me. I thought everybody could jump like that, even though I never actually saw anyone do it. I knew I didn't want them teasing me, so I said, "No, I can't fly." And, to make sure they left me alone, I said, "Johnny must be crazy."

I didn't really mean it. I just wanted those kids to leave me alone. But they started calling him "Crazy Johnny" and teasing him all of the time, and I was too scared and ashamed to defend him, and Johnny got mad and said it was my fault—and then we weren't friends anymore.

And I didn't jump anymore, at least not when anyone was looking. And I learned how to climb a tree and get back down, like the other kids.

Mom never asked me again about jumping, and so it became something I kept to myself and did when I was sure no one else was around. Until I was in junior high.

(Takes a big breath.)

My cousin Elizabeth died. We were about the same age. She lived downtown in an apartment building.

Lizzie and some friends were playing up on top of the apartment building one night, and Lizzie fell off, down five stories, and died. It was the first time someone I knew well, someone my age, had died. Everyone in our family was heartbroken; her parents were in shock. I was kind of—numb.

We went to the funeral, and the kids who were up on the roof with her that night were there, looking sad and sitting alone. Then we went to Lizzie's parents' house to eat and visit and comfort them. Everyone brought some food; it was like a party, only sad. Lizzie's friends were there, too, sitting off in a corner by themselves. Some of the adults would look over at them once in a while, then go back to talking softly with each other.

I asked Mom what was going on, why the kids were alone like that with the adults whispering. She said sometimes adults say mean things. Most of Lizzie's friends were older than her. The adults thought the kids were drinking or doing drugs that night.

Mom said the kids denied that; they said everyone was playing around, and then Lizzie said she could fly. Nobody believed her, and they started teasing her and told her to prove it. They said Lizzie said, "OK," and then she ran and jumped off the edge of the building and fell straight down to the sidewalk.

> *(TERI briefly looks down, wipes their eyes with a hand, then their nose, sniffs, then continues.)*

A couple of kids claimed that Lizzie did say OK, but then when she got over to the ledge, she stopped to look across, and then down, like she was trying to do calculations or something. And then some of them ran over to stop her, and she accidentally got pushed. And then she didn't fly—she just fell.

I asked Mom what she thought was the truth. She said sometimes there is more than one truth, because there are some things you can't tell everyone.

I said, "Do you mean secrets?" She said yes, and she told me that everyone has secrets: some people live an entire lifetime with secrets, some people eventually tell a few trusted friends because some secrets are too powerful to live alone with, and some people are so haunted by their secrets that it kills them.

I asked Mom if all secrets are bad. She said that most secrets seem bad to the one who holds them, and sometimes it's holding on to secrets that causes the most harm. She said that sometimes the best thing is to find someone you trust completely with your life and share that secret with them. If they love you, they will love you in spite of it, or because of it.

I asked her what if it makes them afraid of you and they leave you because of the secret. She said, "It's a chance you take, and it means their friendship may not have been as strong as you thought it was.

But no matter what happens, when you tell someone a secret, the secret loses some of its power over you."

I've never forgotten that. Secrets are hard.

(*Beat.*)

I have shared my secret with a few people I trust the most. Some have not understood it or can't accept it, and they have left me. Some have not understood, but they have accepted it and loved me for sharing it. And some have shared a secret with me. But most of all, that secret is no longer a threat to me; it no longer has power over me. It's no longer something I must keep hidden at all costs, causing me to suffer in unimaginable ways.

Flying is something I can live with now, something I can enjoy, something I can share with someone who knows me and understands me, someone who can appreciate it as a gift, instead of something shameful. Sometimes it starts to get control over me again, but I know how to make it lose its power.

And that's why I'm sharing my secret with you.

(*TERI, still standing, brings feet together, raises arms up high, spreads fingers, looks at the audience and smiles, then looks up, bends at the knees, ready to jump.*)

(*Lights out.*)

END OF PLAY

A MONOGAMY OF SWANS

John Minigan

John Minigan is a recent Massachusetts Cultural Council Artist Fellow in Dramatic Writing and New Repertory Theatre Playwriting Fellow. He has developed new work with Urban Stages, Orlando Shakespeare Theater, Utah Shakespeare Festival, Portland Stage Company, and the Great Plains Theatre Conference. *Queen of Sad Mischance* was a 2020 winner of the New American Voices Festival and the 2019 Clauder Competition. *Noir Hamlet* was a *Boston Globe* Critics' Pick and an *EDGE Media* Best of Boston Theater for 2018. His work is included in the *Best American Short Plays*, *Best Ten-Minute Short Plays*, and *New England New Plays* anthologies, and published by YouthPLAYS, Smith Scripts, and Theatrefolk. He is on the faculties of Emerson College and the Hanover Theatre Conservatory and serves as Dramatists Guild Ambassador for Eastern New England. Website: johnminigan.com.

SYNOPSIS

After breaking up with her fiancé, Jimmie, Ellie has gone to Boston's Public Garden to kill the swans. Her former lover Violet arrives with a better alternative.

CHARACTERS

ELLIE, 20s–30s, a Bostonian.
VIOLET, 20s–30s, a former Bostonian.

SETTING

Boston. The Public Garden near the lagoon.

TIME

A quiet morning in spring.

NOTE

Both characters' accents show their Boston origin.
The city name Haverhill is pronounced "HAYV-ril."

ELLIE throws pieces of bread toward the lagoon. Not gently. In fact, there's murderous intent, an occasional grunt, and a definite snarl.

ELLIE: Come on, you frickin' no-good . . . Come on! Come on!

(She throws harder.)

You little bastards, I'm gonna get you, so help me God. Yeah, you *keep* your distance, you know what's good for you.

(She throws again, then sits and puts her head in her hands.)

VIOLET: (*Off.*) Ellie?

ELLIE: Oh, shit.

VIOLET: (*Off.*) Ellie, is that you down there?

ELLIE: No, it's not me!

VIOLET: (*Off.*) Ellie!

> (*ELLIE stands and winds up to throw again. VIOLET enters.*)

ELLIE: Aw, for crissake!

> (*ELLIE considers the bread, considers VIOLET, then gently tosses a piece toward the lake.*)

What are you doing here?

VIOLET: I tried your apartment first. I figured you were prob'ly here.

ELLIE: How you figure I'm at the Public Garden?

VIOLET: 'Cause I saw Facebook. I figured something was, you know—I figured I better drive down and see what you were doing.

ELLIE: You drove all the way down from Haverhill just to see what I was doing?

VIOLET: 'Cause I saw what you put on Facebook.

> (*VIOLET looks out.*)

That's them?

ELLIE: Little bastards.

VIOLET: You shouldn't put on Facebook you're going to kill them. Wha'd you do, poison the bread?

ELLIE: Don't believe everything you see on the internet, all right? I'm just feeding them.

VIOLET: Why you feeding them if you're gonna kill them?

ELLIE: That is so like you, you know? Asking questions. 'Cause you always gotta have your "information." Well, let me tell you something:

life is not just a bunch of questions. Because if life was just a bunch of questions, you'd spend all your time asking and maybe you'd get an answer and maybe the answer you get wouldn't be good for anybody and you'd realize maybe you should have kept your fat mouth shut.

(ELLIE picks up a rock and prepares to throw it.)

VIOLET: That is a rock.

ELLIE: I know it's a rock.

VIOLET: Are you gonna throw a rock at the swans?

ELLIE: What, you want me to throw it at you?

VIOLET: What have you got against them?

ELLIE: That's another good question. Why don't we ask? Hey, frickin' swans! I'm thinking I might throw this rock and it might hit you, and Vi here would like an explanation as to why I would do that. Do you have an explanation?

(She waits for an answer.)

They got no answer. Filled with secrets. Filled with deception.

VIOLET: I'm sorry about you and Jimmie.

ELLIE: I don't want to talk about Jimmie.

VIOLET: I'm sorry he left.

ELLIE: Oh, yeahyeahyeah, you're prob'ly all broken up about that.

VIOLET: He didn't deserve you.

ELLIE: Is that why you drove down from Haverhill? Because Jimmie didn't deserve me?

VIOLET: I drove down 'cause you put on Facebook how you were going to kill the swans. "The best thing I could do this morning would be to go down the Public Garden and kill the frickin' swans." Who writes "frickin'" on Facebook?

(ELLIE winds up to throw the rock.)

Do not throw the rock! It isn't their fault he left. That was an experiment, you going out with Jimmie.

ELLIE: It was not an experiment.

VIOLET: It was an experiment. You tried it and it didn't work out.

(ELLIE drops the rock on the ground and sits again. VIOLET sits next to her and tries to put her arm around ELLIE's shoulder.)

ELLIE: None of that.

VIOLET: I thought maybe you needed a hug. I didn't mean anything.

ELLIE: You were the experiment, Vi. Not Jimmie.

VIOLET: We were together two years, and that's an experiment?

ELLIE: Then we broke up. I was all set up to marry Jimmie.

VIOLET: You tried, and it didn't work.

ELLIE: You hear Jimmie left, you drive down from Haverhill because you think maybe all of a sudden I'm gonna . . . You know.

VIOLET: I drove down 'cause, you kill these swans, they're gonna lock you up.

ELLIE: I'm feeding them.

(ELLIE tosses a piece of bread.)

VIOLET: You definitely didn't poison the bread?

ELLIE: What kind of a person do you think I am?

VIOLET: I don't know, but they're keeping their distance, now. You see what you did?

ELLIE: For the reception, my mother was gonna have us put swans on the wedding cake. You know, instead of man and wife? Two swans, kissing. You know . . .

(She puts her arms together in a "swan/heart" gesture.)

And she wanted this ice sculpture of swans, only with their bodies all filled up with, like, honeydew melon.

VIOLET: That's nice.

ELLIE: It's not nice. You know how long an ice sculpture's gonna last? You get a swan with a melted neck and a gut full of melon. That's supposed to be romantic? What a stupid woman. A stupid woman with a stupid idea.

VIOLET: It's because they mate for life.

ELLIE: That's the other internet thing that's completely wrong.

VIOLET: What are you talking about?

ELLIE: Swans mating for life. Not true.

VIOLET: That's supposed to be, like, a scientific fact.

ELLIE: Well, the scientists forgot the detail that swans pretty much all look alike. They assumed it was always the same two swans. They screw around like everybody else.

(VIOLET looks out at the lagoon.)

Little bastards!

(ELLIE throws bread at the swans.)

VIOLET: Where'd you hear this?

ELLIE: From Jimmie.

VIOLET: Was he . . . ? You know—

ELLIE: His upstairs neighbor.

VIOLET: Oh, I met that one. I hate her.

ELLIE: And his downstairs neighbor.

VIOLET: No.

ELLIE: Yeah.

VIOLET: I hate her, too.

ELLIE: And that one across the street from him, undoes her top when she tans?

VIOLET: At least, now you know.

ELLIE: And the counter girl at Dunkin' with the side ponytail?

VIOLET: Her?

ELLIE: Her mother.

VIOLET: Jesus.

ELLIE: I said, "We're supposed to get married Thanksgiving. We're supposed to have swans on the wedding cake." "Well, Ellie, you may not be aware of this, but swans, contrary to popular blah blah blah." He saw it on the internet.

VIOLET: That's just what they're like.

ELLIE: So he says.

   (She shouts at the swans.)

You're lousy frickin' role models!

VIOLET: I mean men, Ellie. It's what they're like. He was an experiment. You tried.

ELLIE: Listen, Vi—

VIOLET: Where's Jimmie right now? He must have seen Facebook, right? He knew what you were gonna do and where is he? Did he come down here to make sure you didn't do something terrible?

ELLIE: I would'a thrown the rock at him.

VIOLET: He would'a deserved it. Come here.

(VIOLET sits again. ELLIE sits near her this time.)

You said you thought we shouldn't be together. You met this guy Jimmie, and you thought maybe things were gonna be different. It didn't work out.

ELLIE: Why'd you let me try?

VIOLET: 'Cause I know about us. I know how I feel about you. I figured, you go ahead, try being with a guy, but it's not going to last 'cause I know how you feel about me.

(She puts her arms around ELLIE's shoulder.)

ELLIE: I don't think you and me—

VIOLET: (*Interrupting.*) These swans? I looked them up. They're called Romeo and Juliet.

ELLIE: You looked on the internet?

VIOLET: This one's true.

ELLIE: Well, Juliet's lucky there's just the two of them, 'cause Romeo would be flapping around with all the others.

VIOLET: They're both girls.

ELLIE: What are you talking about?

VIOLET: Seriously. Two girl swans. They've been together, like, ten years.

ELLIE: How do they know this? Swans pretty much all look alike.

VIOLET: They're the same pair.

ELLIE: No kidding. *Massachusetts*, right?

VIOLET: I don't know about mating for life. But ten years. I figure that's pretty good for swans. They know how they feel about each other.

ELLIE: I guess they do.

VIOLET: Gimme some of that.

ELLIE: I scared them off, they're not gonna—

VIOLET: Just gimme some.

(ELLIE gives VIOLET some bread. VIOLET stands and walks to the edge of the water. She makes kissing sounds to attract the swans. ELLIE stands and walks to a spot beside her.)

ELLIE: You drove down all the way from Haverhill just so I wouldn't do something stupid?

VIOLET: Yeah, I did. Look, look, look. They're coming in.

(She is about to toss bread to them. ELLIE blocks her arm.)

ELLIE: Maybe you better not do that.

VIOLET: Why not?

(Pause. VIOLET looks at the bread in her hand.)

No, you didn't really. Did you?

(Pause. ELLIE smiles a little.)

ELLIE: Of course I didn't. What kind of person do you think I am?

(ELLIE slips her hand into VIOLET's. VIOLET smiles.)

END OF PLAY

ON THE PORCH

Debbie Lamedman

Debbie Lamedman is a playwright, editor, and teaching artist currently living in Portland, Oregon. Her books and plays have been published by Smith & Kraus, Inc. and Heuer Publishing. In addition to writing, Debbie has worked as an adjunct theater instructor and guest director at Pacific University, Portland Actors Conservatory, and Portland Center Stage. Debbie received her MFA in theater from Brandeis University and is a proud member of the Dramatists Guild, and a member of Honor Roll!, an advocacy group of women and playwrights over forty. Many of Debbie's scripts are available on her New Play Exchange profile (newplayexchange.org). Website: debbielamedman.com.

SYNOPSIS

Sylvie is getting high on her porch when her neighbor Jean stops by for a chat. What starts as a brief neighborly conversation quickly becomes two women baring their souls to one another as they commiserate over their anxieties of aging in this youth-conscious society.

CHARACTERS

SYLVIE, approaching her 60th birthday. She has run out of steam, depressed. She is both lonely and wants to isolate. She is trying to come to terms with the changes in her body, and the changes in her life, and the world around her.

JEAN, Sylvie's neighbor, a few years younger in mid-to-late 50s. Jean accepts things as they are. She's not one to ruffle feathers. She doesn't give any thought to whether or not she is happy. This is the way things are.

SETTING

The porch of a 1925 Craftsman house in Portland, Oregon.

TIME

Midmorning in late summer.
A weekday. Probably a Wednesday.
Before the pandemic . . . so, summer 2019.

At rise: a sunny, cool midmorning in late summer. Fall is on the way. SYLVIE is sitting in an Adirondack chair on the porch of her house. She is watching two squirrels frolic in the tree in her front yard. SYLVIE is smoking pot out of a glass pipe. She is relaxed and feeling slightly blissful. SYLVIE breathes in and smiles as she watches the squirrels chase each other around the trunk of the tree. She is enjoying the breeze.

SYLVIE: (*Sings off-key to Pink Floyd's "Breathe."*) Breathe. Breathe in the air . . .

> (*JEAN, SYLVIE's neighbor from across the street, approaches. At first, we don't see JEAN as she stands outside of SYLVIE's yard.*)

JEAN: (*Off.*) Hi there, stranger!

(SYLVIE waves.)

(Off.) How ya been? Haven't seen you in a while.

SYLVIE: I've been hiding.

JEAN: *(Off.)* Yeah, you have. *(Beat.)* Still hiding?

SYLVIE: Not entirely.

JEAN: *(Off.)* May I join you?

    (Beat. SYLVIE hesitates.)

(Off.) I won't stay long.

SYLVIE: Sure. Come on up.

    (JEAN enters. Sits in another Adirondack chair next to SYLVIE.)

I was watching the show.

JEAN: What show?

SYLVIE: The squirrel show. Two of 'em chasing each other round the tree. So cute.

JEAN: It's only cute if they're not invading your attic.

SYLVIE: Oh no! Did they?

JEAN: Last year. Didn't I tell you? We had a whole family up there. Not cute.

SYLVIE: Oh, that's right. I remember.

JEAN: Carl kept saying, "It's better than rats," but I don't think so. Rodents are rodents!

SYLVIE: Well, we have a deal, the squirrels and me. I don't bother them if they stay outside, and they're not allowed to come into my house and bother me! Same deal with the spiders!

JEAN: Tell me about it!

(*Slightly awkward beat.*)

Stella helps keep the squirrels at bay, doesn't she?

(*Beat.*)

SYLVIE: Who?

JEAN: (*Laughing.*) Stella? Your dog?

(*SYLVIE cracks up laughing. The pot has caught up to her.*)

SYLVIE: Oh yeah. Stella. (*Yells out à la Stanley Kowalski.*) STELLAAAAAAAAAA!

(*JEAN is a little taken aback.*)

JEAN: You're stoned.

SYLVIE: Indeed I am. Only way to pass the time these days.

JEAN: Life's got you down, huh?

SYLVIE: You have no idea.

(*Awkward beat.*)

(*SYLVIE takes another hit off her pipe. Does not offer any to JEAN.*)

JEAN: It's so nice out here. You get such a lovely breeze.

SYLVIE: This porch is my favorite thing about this house. You can smell fall. It's on its way. Can't wait.

JEAN: I like the summer.

SYLVIE: I hate it. Now more than ever. It seems to be hotter every year. And the bugs. They drive me nuts.

JEAN: Agreed. I'm not a fan either.

SYLVIE: Umm-hmmm.

(Beat.)

JEAN: Syl?

SYLVIE: Yeah?

JEAN: Are you upset with me for any reason?

SYLVIE: Why? Why would I be?

JEAN: I don't know. You're acting . . . I just haven't seen you in so long and I wondered if—

SYLVIE: *(Bluntly.)* We're not that close.

JEAN: *(Scoffs.)* Yes, I realize that. But we are neighbors. And you seem . . . aloof.

SYLVIE: I'm high.

JEAN: Is that all?

SYLVIE: Mmm-hmm. *(Beat.)* Did you want some?

JEAN: Oh! No! It's a little early, isn't it?

SYLVIE: Not for me. What else do I have going on?

JEAN: Syl . . .

SYLVIE: *(Handing the pipe and lighter to JEAN.)* Go ahead. I won't tell.

JEAN: *(Refuses the pipe.)* No. I . . . I don't . . . I don't do that.

SYLVIE: Why not?

JEAN: I don't need it.

SYLVIE: Oh . . . you don't *need* it.

JEAN: No. I've never done it and I'm not going to start now.

SYLVIE: I see. *(Beat.)* Let me ask you something?

JEAN: Sure.

SYLVIE: Do you *need* that glass or two of wine every night?

JEAN: Excuse me?

SYLVIE: I'm just saying, Jean . . . don't judge me for smoking pot, and I won't judge you for having a coupla drinks every night.

JEAN: I wasn't judging you.

SYLVIE: Oh. Okay. Right.

JEAN: I wasn't. I just don't want any.

SYLVIE: Fair enough.

(Awkward beat. Almost spitefully, SYLVIE takes another hit.)

JEAN: Are you okay?

SYLVIE: Why wouldn't I be?

JEAN: Look, you don't have to tell me anything if you don't want to . . . but you said you've been hiding, and I haven't seen you all summer. Now, here you are, out on the porch in the morning smoking weed. Something's going on.

SYLVIE: I have constant headaches. The weed helps.

JEAN: Have you seen a doctor?

SYLVIE: I have burning inside. Not heartburn . . . fire! Inside me. Not summer heat. Burning-from-inside-my-body heat. The weed helps.

JEAN: Again, have you gone to the doctor?

SYLVIE: Don't need to.

JEAN: It sounds like you do.

SYLVIE: Nope. I know what's going on.

JEAN: Do you want to talk about it?

(Beat.)

SYLVIE: How old are you, Jean?

(Beat. JEAN laughs self-consciously.)

JEAN: Uh . . . I hate saying the number out loud.

SYLVIE: I know what you mean.

JEAN: I'm sure I'm older than you.

SYLVIE: Don't bet on it.

JEAN: I'm uh . . . I'm fifty.

SYLVIE: Ah . . . fifty.

(Beat.)

JEAN: It's not so bad.

SYLVIE: Not yet. Just you wait, little Missy.

JEAN: How old are you? Same, right?

SYLVIE: Nope.

JEAN: Come on.

SYLVIE: My birthday is next month, Jean.

JEAN: Oh! Wonderful! Are you doing anything special?

SYLVIE: Turning sixty, Jean! That's pretty damn special, dontcha think?

JEAN: You are not!

SYLVIE: Wanna see my driver's license?

(Beat.)

JEAN: I had no idea. I really thought you were in your forties.

SYLVIE: That's a crock of shit, Jean.

JEAN: What? No! You really look great.

SYLVIE: For sixty.

JEAN: No, Sylvie. Don't put words in my mouth. I'm sorry you're having such a hard time with it.

SYLVIE: You will too. It starts in a few years after you turn fifty.

JEAN: Isn't fifty the new thirty?

SYLVIE: Fifty is fifty! Sixty is sixty! I don't care how a person looks or feels for that matter! The truth is the body knows! And it starts to go. Plastic surgery cannot fool Mother Nature.

JEAN: Well, I think you look great!

SYLVIE: (*Starting to ramp up.*) Thank you, Jean, but you obviously haven't been paying attention.

JEAN: What are you talking about?

> (*SYLVIE starts off slowly; by the end of the monologue, she is utterly ramped up.*)

SYLVIE: I have put on quite a bit of weight in the past few years. I eat my blueberries. I eat my broccoli. I take long walks several times a day with my dog. Doesn't matter. I cannot lose weight. My breasts have grown and changed shape so much, I can't find a bra to support or fit me. My stomach feels like it's down to my knees. My belly is now so big, pools of sweat form underneath it and frankly, it stinks. Literally. Baby powder does not seem to take the stench away. This odor. Under my belly. Under my breasts. It's like old gym socks. I'm mildewing. My personal hygiene is just fine, but my body chemistry has changed, and I don't smell good anymore. I certainly don't smell like I used to, that's for sure. I used to smell good. I *used to be* known for my lovely scent.

I suppose the worst part is I have no sex drive. None. And even if I did, I'm so dried up down there, it actually hurts to be touched. And the itchiness. Have I mentioned the itchiness? Continuous, but mostly at night. At night, when I'm *not* sleeping because I can no longer sleep, I want to rip out my crotch and throw it across the room!

(*Pause.*)

Did you know any of these things, Jean?

JEAN: You're scaring me.

SYLVIE: Good! You should be scared! No matter what you do, all these things will happen. I'm telling you, whatever your genetic makeup is, or your yearly income, it's coming to get you. Jane Fonda looks amazing, but you can't tell me she doesn't get out of bed every morning groaning from all her aches and pains.

(*SYLVIE takes a deep breath and lets it out audibly. She adds more pot to the pipe and takes a hit. JEAN is looking hard at SYLVIE. SYLVIE looks straight ahead, lost in her thoughts.*)

(*Beat.*)

JEAN: (*Quietly.*) I'm not fifty.

(*Beat. SYLVIE turns to JEAN.*)

SYLVIE: What?

JEAN: I lied. I'm so used to lying. It's so dumb.

SYLVIE: How old are you?

JEAN: (*Clearing her throat.*) Fifty-six.

(*SYLVIE smiles and nods her head.*)

SYLVIE: Shaved off six years. How does that make you feel?

JEAN: (*Laughing.*) At this age, it hardly makes a difference.

SYLVIE: Agreed.

JEAN: I'm going through everything you described. Everything! I don't feel quite like myself anymore.

SYLVIE: Nobody ever really tells you what to expect.

JEAN: No. They don't. I thought I was pregnant.

SYLVIE: Oh, good God. Now *that's* naive, Jean.

JEAN: I mean, obviously I knew this change was coming, but I had no idea it was . . .

SYLVIE: This.

(They both start laughing. Then quiet. Reflecting.)

JEAN: It sure feels good to laugh. I've been doing nothing but crying for days.

SYLVIE: I know. And I feel petty complaining about it, considering everything else there is to cry about in this world. I'm just getting old . . . no big deal.

JEAN: But it is a big deal. We're losing ourselves . . .

SYLVIE: Fading . . .

JEAN: Yes . . .

(SYLVIE once again reaches for her pipe. Both women are staring straight ahead, lost in thought. SYLVIE lights up the pipe. She turns to JEAN and offers it. JEAN takes the pipe and lights it. Lights fade.)

END OF PLAY

ORBITING THE SUN

Sara Jean Accuardi

Sara Jean Accuardi is an award-winning playwright and the recipient of the 2021 Oregon Literary Arts Leslie Bradshaw Fellowship for Drama. Her full-length plays include *The Delays*, *BREAK*, *The Storyteller*, *< 3*, *Love Scenes*, and *Portrait of the Widow Kinski*. Her writing has been produced and developed around the country, including with Theatre Vertigo, Seven Devils Playwrights Conference, Something Marvelous, Victory Gardens, Portland Center Stage, Chicago Dramatists, The Blank Theatre, Spooky Action Theater, and PlayMakers Repertory Company. *The Storyteller* won the 2020 International Thomas Wolfe Playwriting Competition, and *The Delays* received the 2019 Drammy Award for Outstanding Original Script. She has been a finalist for the O'Neill National Playwrights Conference and the Oregon Book Awards. Sara Jean holds an MFA in writing for the screen and stage from Northwestern University and is a member of the Dramatists Guild and LineStorm Playwrights. Her plays are available on her New Play Exchange profile. Website: sarajeanaccuardi.com.

SYNOPSIS

A mother and son do their best to mark the passage of time.

CHARACTERS

MOM, 40s–60s.
SON, 20s.

SETTING

A front porch.

TIME

Evening.

A front porch.
It's late.
It's dark.
It has been raining.
A single brightly colored balloon is tied to a railing.
MOM sits on the front steps, holding a coffee mug.
She waits for a long time. She's not happy.
She pops the balloon and waits some more.
SON hurries to the stoop. He carries a cake box.

SON: I'm so sorry.

> *(MOM shrugs.)*

I didn't forget. Everything took longer than— Why do people talk so much? It was so clear everyone wanted to leave, but, instead, we just stood there awkwardly chatting in the doorway, trapped in endless small talk— Why are you out here?

MOM: To surprise you.

SON: Very surprising.

MOM: To welcome you, I guess.

SON: How long have you been waiting?

MOM: Not long.

SON: Yeah?

MOM: You brought a cake.

SON: Well, it's left over from—

MOM: Oh.

SON: Are we going inside?

MOM: Thought we'd stay out here a bit.

SON: It's cold.

MOM: This isn't cold.

SON: Okay.

(He puts the cake box down.)

MOM: Didn't know they'd have a cake.

SON: Pretty standard.

MOM: Thought that was my traditional birthday contribution.

SON: I can have multiple cakes.

MOM: I know.

SON: Okay. So.

MOM: Is Lisa coming?

SON: She works early, so I thought—

MOM: Oh, right. That's okay.

SON: Let's head inside.

MOM: Just a little longer.

(They sit in silence.)

Happy birthday. Forgot to say that.

SON: Thanks.

(More silence.)

MOM: Did you know the Barnetts still do things together? Holidays, vacations even—them, the kids, new spouses—they're all this big happy extended family. Friends.

A lot of people do that. Don't you think that's incredible?

SON: No.

MOM: It's amazing to me.

SON: Didn't Jane Barnett go to jail or something?

MOM: I'm not saying—

SON: That family's a mess.

MOM: I'm just pointing out that they all get along. It's nice. For the kids.

SON: But the kids are all screwed up too.

MOM: You know what I mean.

SON: No. I don't.

MOM: Okay.

(Silence.)

SON: Sorry. Just—I imagine there are some better examples out there.

MOM: Probably.

SON: And you guys do okay. We always work it out.

MOM: I guess.

SON: Today got a little crowded. But I made it, right?

(*MOM doesn't respond.*)

(*Re: the mug.*) Coffee?

MOM: Hot chocolate.

SON: Hm.

MOM: I don't want to be depressing.

SON: You're not.

MOM: Needy.

SON: You're not.

MOM: Did you check your messages? You should.

(*SON looks at his phone.*)

SON: You called a lot.

MOM: Yes.

SON: Fifteen missed calls.

MOM: See? That's crazy. You're twenty-three. Why can't I let you enjoy your birthday? Was it good? Lisa's parents, then Dad—anything else?

SON: Lisa and I went out for a bit.

MOM: That's nice.

SON: Next year we'll start with you. I promise.

MOM: It's not about that.

SON: It's important to me, though. I wanted to be here.

MOM: How's the cake?

SON: Eh.

MOM: I'm sure it's great.

SON: It's covered in that fondant crap.

MOM: Fancy.

SON: Yeah, but you can't eat it.

MOM: Yes, you can.

SON: It's gross.

MOM: Agreed.

SON: I'm glad you're a firm believer in buttercream.

MOM: Amen.

   (MOM smiles. Then doesn't.)

Birthdays are the worst, aren't they? Everyone grabbing for your attention. I don't mean to add to the stress.

SON: (*A joke.*) Yeah, you do.

MOM: I'm dragging you into my crap, and that's not fair.

SON: It's my crap too.

MOM: No. Your world is getting bigger, and I need to accept that. This isn't the center anymore, and that's a good thing. How it should be. Healthy. You've got a lot going on—Lisa, friends—I spend all this time trying to figure out where I fit in, and the simple truth is I don't. I'm not supposed to. But still, I try and try until I become this black hole that's determined to pull you back, and I'm sorry.

I'm so sorry.

SON: You're my mom. That's your job, right?

MOM: My job is to let you go.

SON: . . . You know what I miss?

MOM: What?

SON: Orbiting the sun.

MOM: Pretty sure we're still doing that.

SON: I'm serious. When did we stop that ritual?

MOM: When you were five.

SON: We did it longer than that. I was, like, sixteen.

MOM: Not that old.

SON: At least fourteen. I was old enough for it to be super embarrassing, I distinctly remember that.

MOM: The numbers started to get too high. I would have made you continue otherwise.

SON: I'm sure.

MOM: I'm glad you remember it fondly.

SON: Well. It did make a birthday feel complete.

   (. . .)

Can I do it?

MOM: No.

SON: Please. A trip around the sun for each year of my life.

MOM: You're too old.

   (*MOM stands.*)

I'm going in. I'll get your cake.

(SON stands and walks a quick circle around his mother.)

SON: One.

MOM: Stop.

(Another circle.)

SON: Two.

MOM: Come on.

(Another.)

SON: Three.

MOM: You're not—

SON: Four.

MOM: —doing this twenty-three—

SON: Five.

MOM: —times.

SON: Six. You're supposed to do the counting, Mom.

(MOM heads for the door. SON stops her.)

MOM: Excuse me.

SON: Seventeen to go.

MOM: You need help.

SON: It's genetic. Seven.

(A circle.)

Eight.

(A circle.)

Nine.

(A circle.)

Ten.

(MOM slowly sits down.)

Eleven.

(He circles again.)

MOM: Twelve.

(Again.)

Thirteen.

(Again.)

Fourteen.

(Again.)

Fifteen.

(Again.)

Sixteen.

(Again.)

Seventeen.

(Another orbit.)

SON: I love you.

MOM: I love you too.

(He continues to orbit as she counts.)

END OF PLAY

SCREAM

George Sapio

George Sapio is an award-winning playwright, director, producer, actor, and dramaturg. He produces and hosts *Onstage/Offstage*, a radio show/podcast (est. 2013) featuring interviews with theater professionals from around the world (onstageoffstage.org). His book *Workshopping the New Play: A Guide for Playwrights, Directors, and Dramaturgs* is published by Applause Books. He was founder and artistic director of the Ithaca Fringe Festival and a photojournalist whose book *Collateral Damage*, written with his wife, features his pictures and essays from two trips to Iraq in 2003. Find his plays on the New Play Exchange (newplayexchange.org). Website: gsapio.com.

SYNOPSIS

One person's therapy is another's torture. Woody attempts to dump angst into the Existential Void . . . but finds that it's occupied. And not receptive at all.

CHARACTERS

WOODY, self-involved. Cast as appropriate.
THE UNIVERSE, fed up. Called the "Voice." Offstage. Cast as
   appropriate.

SETTING

A lonely field.

TIME

Midnight.

NOTE

Slashes / indicate dialogue overlap.

*A lonely field. Midnight. WOODY runs on, stops center stage, inhales,
ready to scream.*

VOICE: Umm . . . no.

   (WOODY looks around, perplexed. Inhales again.)

I said no.

WOODY: What?

VOICE: Don't do that.

WOODY: Do what?

VOICE: Really?

WOODY: Who are you?

VOICE: The Universe.

WOODY: What? Where are you?

VOICE: Hiding.

WOODY: What? I don't understand.

VOICE: Okay. It was a joke. Sorry. A bad one. Let me make this simple in the hopes that you will go away. You're here in the middle of nowhere, getting ready to scream in extreme soul-suffering agony.

WOODY: What? Who *are* you?

VOICE: I'm . . . (Oh boy.) I'm The Universe.

WOODY: I must be having a really bad dream.

VOICE: Exactly. You're in a bad dream. In fact, you're in a bad dream with a snarky, pissed-off voice who really does not want to hear your self-indulgent yuppie existential angst hissy fit. So pack it up, roll over, touch yourself, go for a pee or whatever it is you need to do. Okay?

WOODY: Who *are* you?

VOICE: (*Muttering.*) Humans. Someone had to think them up. (*Clears throat. In a bold voice:*) I am Everything. I am immeasurably small and incalculably huge. I am all colors. I am all sounds. I am all numbers, be they negative, positive, or irrational. I am every single beginning, and I am the End of All Things. I am every past ever recorded and every conceivable future. My right hand is unimaginable light and my left, unending, absolute darkness. I am every being ever conceived. I am so massive that your world is no more than a grain of sand stuck to a crab's asshole buried on a beach the size of your own solar system. And that solar system is in my spare change bowl. (*Beat.*) Just go with it, okay?

WOODY: I'm not going with . . . that! That's stupid.

VOICE: Nice.

WOODY: Come on. Where are you? I'm having a bad day here. Tell me the truth and stop messing with me.

VOICE: I am telling you the truth. I'm everywhere and I'm Everything.

WOODY: You're God?

VOICE: (*Emphatically.*) No.

WOODY: No.

VOICE: I'm not "God."

WOODY: So then if you're Everything, where's God?

VOICE: In your head, that's where.

WOODY: Shows what you know. I was told—on good authority—that God is everywhere.

VOICE: On whose good authority? I only ask because you are out here in the middle of nowhere ready to let loose with a cry of anguish. And you are, by the way, did I forget to mention it . . . speaking to The Everything.

WOODY: You're The Everything?

VOICE: I'm the genuine goods, babe. Here, There, and Everywhere.

WOODY: And a Beatles fan.

VOICE: Doesn't get much better than that. Except maybe Green Day.

WOODY: Why are you talking to me, then? Aren't there a billion other universes you need to attend to?

VOICE: Not really. No. Actually there are only about four thousand, three hundred and sixty-two that need attention. Yours is one of the most troublesome. And I'm speaking to you because I'm completely spent having had to listen to you humanoids and your insufferable whining.

WOODY: Humanoids.

VOICE: Yes.

WOODY: Whining.

VOICE: I hate to break it to you, but you humans? You're a mistake of nature. Once in about . . . no, never mind. That number would make your head explode. Once in a very, very, very, *very* huge off chance, humanoids come into being. And in every single case they manage—somehow—to make whatever world they find to breed in a complete disaster.

WOODY: Well, Mr. Everything certainly has no shortage on massive attitude, that's for sure. Look. All I wanted was one good scream. One chance to let out some of the frustration I have pent up inside. I need some release, dammit!

   (Opens mouth to scream.)

VOICE: I swear. If you do that, I will let out the flying monkeys and whomp your pathetic ass big time.

WOODY: Omigod. You are completely without mercy.

VOICE: Look who's talking!

WOODY: You just do not like humans at all.

VOICE: Lemme explain something to you. You're a chimp with a credit card. Your species has no idea whatsoever the place you hold in the grand scheme of things. You know that one three-year-old who has no idea how to act in concert with its classmates? Who never stops whining? Who never stops attracting attention to itself? Who has no concept of anything other than its own—unjustified, may I add—self-importance? That's humans.

WOODY: So what? We're, like, one planet in a billion galaxies. (*Silence.*) We're not? (*Silence.*) Omigod.

VOICE: Pay attention. You humanoids aren't much in the overall picture. But I'm picky and easily pissed off. And yes, there are more of you out there.

WOODY: How many?

VOICE: None of your business. None of you will most likely ever get to know each other. And if you did, it would be a bigger mess than the ones you already make on your own backwater planets.

WOODY: I don't understand. Are we that many? No? Then what's the problem? If, as you say, there aren't that many of us out there, then how can one scream be so annoying? You that touchy?

VOICE: I'm going to explain this. Once. Do you have any idea how much noise there is all through the void? Aside from the background noise of the initial expansion, almost none. And I'm used to it. It's background, and it's fading. It's quiet here. Amongst billions of galaxies there really isn't much noise. Yes, occasionally a red giant gets sucked into a black hole, but that's more amusing than bothersome. Otherwise, it's all debris. Carbon-based detritus . . . ice . . . rock. Drifting. Making its way through the dark matter. Doing nothing. It's peaceful. All in all, there's not much life out there.

WOODY: But the vastness. Isn't that enough to bury the sound of the occasional cry of angst?

VOICE: Not really. Your planet alone, between its endless cries of despair and agony, and its nonstop episodes of war, makes enough noise all on its own to drive me crazy.

WOODY: I'm not believing that.

VOICE: Remove humanoids from the algorithms and the universe is a quiet place. It has to be. Think of the size. See if your tiny brain can attempt to contemplate the trillions of galaxies, each with trillions of stars and orbiting bodies around you.

WOODY: I get it, I get it. It's pretty big, right?

VOICE: Yes. Pretty big. You nailed it. (*Sotto voce.*) It never stops.

WOODY: So then you have room for one scream. I think you're being selfish.

VOICE: But it's not one scream. It's millions. Billions. Dare I mention trillions? Humans do not simply scream and move on. They scream and they keep screaming. And many of you enjoy the screaming so much you keep making everyone around you do it. Yes, there is almost uncountable space and, yes, there should be room for it . . . but really, there isn't.

WOODY: Well, I'm sorry that "The Universe" can't accommodate a raised voice or two. But I have a right to express my own despair. And you have no right to insist that I refrain from what my personal tranquility counselor recommends as a healthful release. My pain is important and needs to be resolved.

VOICE: Has the concept of compassion ever entered your world?

WOODY: Has it ever entered yours? Maybe you should listen to your own words.

VOICE: Excuse me?

WOODY: You keep talking about how humans make noise. Instead of being angry, maybe you should learn to accept that. So what if we are noisy? That's who we are, and we have a right to be that way. As you said, The Universe is a big place, and it should be able to accommodate everyone's needs. I'm sorry if you find it annoying, but we have to be who we are, and you need to accept that.

VOICE: I do?

WOODY: We may not be your idea of perfect, but you have to realize that we are entitled to our own particular nature, which includes emotions, and to try and change us is wrong.

VOICE: Okay. Please. Please listen to me. You need to stop right now.

WOODY: No. I will not stop. I have a right to say what I think.

VOICE: Please. Seriously. Shut up.

WOODY: I will not shut up. I am right.

VOICE: You have no idea what you're doing. I beg you.

WOODY: Maybe you should understand that you have a problem that needs addressing.

VOICE: I cannot believe this.

WOODY: If we are one of the few life forms, then we have rights. We have choices. And if I want to express myself, you have no right to stop me.

VOICE: I'm The Universe.

WOODY: So what?

VOICE: Please. Last chance. Please. Don't push me anymore.

(*WOODY inhales deeply and lets out a hellacious howl of anger and frustration.*)

WOODY: Wow. That was so cleansing. So therapeutic. Every time I do that, I feel better.

VOICE: I asked you not to.

WOODY: Oh well. I did it. Ha-ha. You should try it. (*Silence.*) You should really get over your problem. (*Silence.*) My counselor encourages scream therapy. She says it's a homeopathic way to achieve balance.

VOICE: Does she?

WOODY: She says that screaming releases muscle tension. A really good scream affects every single part of the body, from the toes to the brain, loosening up muscles and releasing endorphins.

VOICE: Yes. Actually I / know that—

WOODY: And every time the body resets, it's as if it were starting over. Completely. That's important. I needed a release. And now I feel calm.

VOICE: Yes. Would you like to know / how I know it?

WOODY: Maybe you should take a lesson from a helpful life form. I'm right about this. I know these things.

VOICE: You're right. Maybe I should. I'm curious: how often do you exercise this total body release?

WOODY: I try to have a full-body scream at least once a month. And you know what? My orgasms are so much better.

VOICE: You just told The Universe about your orgasms.

WOODY: Omigod! Well, it's a good thing. Wow. So the whole universe knows I have great orgasms?

VOICE: Remember what I said? I am The Universe. You are speaking to all of me. Every planet. Every galaxy.

WOODY: That is so fucked up. Wow!

VOICE: Maybe a reset is exactly what I need. Make my problems go away.

WOODY: That's exactly what I was telling you! Wait. How do you mean? What problems?

VOICE: We'll get to that. My pre-scream inhalation, so to speak, pulls all of the matter everywhere together, and I condense to the size of a basketball, which believe me, is extremely uncomfortable. Think of it: all that matter in that small of a space? I reach close to two trillion degrees Fahrenheit and become about as dense as dense can possibly be. Then comes *my* scream: a universe of energy released in an expansion so powerful that, in the first few trillionths of a second, nothing exists but the most basic elements. You have no idea how good it feels to expand and cool down. As you said: calm. Reset. Oh. And if *I* had orgasms? They'd be fucking brilliant.

WOODY: But . . . wait. Wouldn't that . . . I mean what would happen to everything if you . . . ? Shrank?

VOICE: Contracted, actually. The molecules in your body would be packed together so tightly that eight million of you would fit inside a normal-sized carbon atom.

WOODY: But—

VOICE: I assume you're only worried about the consequences to yourself.

WOODY: But—everything?

VOICE: Yes?

WOODY: I mean, what would . . . everything?

VOICE: I'm sorry. I thought you were addressing me directly.

WOODY: But . . . you wouldn't. Right? I mean, everything would die.

VOICE: Well, I wouldn't. I'd simply reset. And I *am* Everything, including your life. So, technically, no. Think of it as complete and total homeopathic therapy.

WOODY: You can't do that!

VOICE: But what about *my* pain? Doesn't it matter? What should I do about it?

WOODY: I have a right to live!

VOICE: Listen. When I said humanoids were few, I was correct. You are mathematically negligible. But I am Everything and that means I am also you. I hear—I feel—all of your screams, all of your cries for pity that you ignore from each other. But I cannot ignore. I hear every one of your war cries. I experience all of your crimes committed against each other. I am not only the bullets you fire but also the bodies they penetrate. Everything that happens to any one of you happens to me. You are indeed few, but you are certainly more than enough. And I am in so much pain. So, yes, thank you. I will take your knowledgeable advice. Because I too have a right to release my pain.

(House lights to black.)

WOODY: Wait! Wait! You're kidding, right?

END OF PLAY

SEEDS

Scott Mullen

Scott Mullen is a longtime Hollywood screenplay analyst and screenwriter, a two-time winner of Amazon Studios' screenwriting contest, whose thrillers *The Summoning, In Broad Daylight*, and *Blood on Her Badge* aired on TV One. His short plays have been produced hundreds of times around the world. An evening of his comic plays, *A NIGHT OF S.M.*, had a two-week run in Hollywood.

SYNOPSIS

A woman is surprised when a teenage girl joins her on a park bench. She's even more surprised when the teen tells her why she is there.

CHARACTERS

DIANE, late 30s–50s. A friendly woman on a park bench.
GWEN, teens. A teenage girl.
JACK, late 30s–50s. Gwen's father.

SETTING

A park bench.

TIME

The present.

NOTE

If for whatever reason the birdseed is a problem, it can be mimed. The pigeons are imaginary.

DIANE sits on a park bench, a small paper bag in her hand. She doesn't notice when GWEN comes in and watches her. DIANE pulls out a handful of birdseed from the bag and tosses it as far away from herself as she can. She watches it land. Smiles. Sees GWEN.

DIANE: The pigeons are hungry today.

GWEN: I guess so.

(DIANE looks at GWEN. GWEN stares back. It's an odd moment.)

DIANE: Do you want to sit down?

(GWEN sits on the bench. DIANE offers her the bag.)

Take a handful of the food and try to toss it as far away from the bench as you can. Don't get it too close. I made that mistake once—I tossed it on the ground down there, and the birds were all over me. I like birds, but not that much. Here.

(GWEN reaches in a hand and pulls out a fistful of food. She opens her hand and looks at it.)

GWEN: What are you feeding them?

DIANE: Dried peas, some wheat, mostly seeds. A lot of people feed them old bread, but that's not very good for them. They like this better.

(GWEN throws the food in the same direction DIANE did.)

Nice throw. Look at them eat. My name's Diane. What's yours?

GWEN: It's silly.

DIANE: There are no silly names.

GWEN: My name is Guinevere.

DIANE: I love that name!

GWEN: No one can spell it.

DIANE: I bet they call you Gwen.

GWEN: They do.

DIANE: That's a nice name too.

(DIANE catches GWEN staring at her again.)

Do we know each other?

GWEN: No. Not really.

DIANE: Not really?

GWEN: Can I throw some more?

(DIANE offers her the bag. GWEN pulls out another fistful. Holds it.)

You love animals, huh?

DIANE: I do.

GWEN: I bet you have pets.

DIANE: Three cats.

GWEN: Three. Wow.

DIANE: You?

GWEN: Not right now. Your kids must like the cats, huh?

DIANE: No kids.

GWEN: Your husband?

DIANE: No husband.

GWEN: Never?

DIANE: Don't let anyone tell you that you need to be married. Or have kids.

GWEN: No, I know.

DIANE: It's not good or bad. It's how life worked out.

GWEN: But you wish you had kids?

DIANE: Sometimes.

GWEN: My mother died when I was four.

DIANE: I'm sorry.

GWEN: I barely remember her. Isn't that awful? I've seen photos, but most of my memories of her are from those photos. Not of us together.

DIANE: You were young.

GWEN: I suppose. It was a car accident. Not her fault. Drunk driver.

DIANE: That's terrible.

GWEN: Yeah.

(GWEN throws the fistful of food. She runs her hands on her legs over and over again, stressed.)

DIANE: Are you okay?

GWEN: I can't do this.

DIANE: Do what?

GWEN: I mean, it's not fair to you. It's going to change things forever, no matter what happens. And maybe that's a good thing, and maybe it isn't. It's a lot of responsibility.

DIANE: What's the matter, Gwen?

(GWEN looks at DIANE.)

GWEN: Are you happy? Really happy?

(DIANE hesitates.)

DIANE: That's a tough question.

GWEN: I know.

DIANE: I guess I am. Sometimes. I'm content. I've made my life.

GWEN: Do you ever dream?

DIANE: Of course.

GWEN: What did you dream last night?

(DIANE smiles.)

What?

DIANE: Last night I dreamed of bears.

GWEN: Bears!

DIANE: In fact, I guess I was a bear. Big and furry. I was traveling with a bunch of bears. We were all going to our caves for the winter to hibernate. And we all had different caves. Which was sort of lonely . . . But I could look out the opening to my cave and see the other bears, looking out their caves, and it felt like we were watching over each other. Strange, I know. Maybe that's why I feed the pigeons. Not everyone likes pigeons. I do.

(DIANE throws some more food.)

GWEN: That's really nice.

DIANE: What do you dream of?

GWEN: Sometimes I dream of different universes. Different lives. Where things didn't work out the same. Do you ever have that dream?

DIANE: Maybe.

GWEN: I want to tell you a story. Let's say it's . . . a story I'm writing for school. And I need an ending. Maybe you can help me with that.

DIANE: I'm listening.

GWEN: It's about a man whose wife dies. And he's really sad, and his children are really sad. And he becomes obsessed with somehow bringing her back. He's a scientist, and he has a lot of stuff in his garage. And he believes there are other universes, parallel universes. And in some his wife didn't die, and she is happy with her family in that world, and he doesn't want to mess with that. And in some she did die, and that's sad too. But maybe, just maybe, there's a parallel universe where she never met him. Where she's living alone, and she thinks she's happy, but maybe she isn't. Because she never met her soulmate. Never met her kids. Never really had that choice.

DIANE: Wow.

GWEN: How do you think that story should end?

DIANE: I guess maybe he finds the woman and talks to her, and if they are soulmates, really soulmates, she can sense that and . . . I don't know. Is he going to stay there with her?

GWEN: I think he'd want her to go back to his universe.

DIANE: So she'd be leaving everything in her world. Everyone.

GWEN: Yes. Though some of those people would exist in the other world.

DIANE: Where she's suddenly alive.

GWEN: It's a tricky story.

DIANE: I like the story. How does it end?

GWEN: I don't know yet. But do you think it can be real? Do you believe it?

DIANE: I don't know. It's pretty far out. But the world is a strange place.

GWEN: There's another wrinkle. Maybe the man is shy. And scared. He finds the woman, and she's single, but he doesn't want to screw it up. He doesn't know if he can talk to her without breaking down—and that might freak her out. So he sends his oldest daughter, the sensible one, the serious one, to try and talk to the woman instead. To feel her out, to see if there's a chance.

DIANE: Wow. You have some imagination.

GWEN: No, I don't. I really don't. I wish I could make this stuff up.

DIANE: I don't understand.

GWEN: Don't freak out. Please. Don't. But I'm your daughter.

DIANE: What?

GWEN: Yeah.

DIANE: I think I'd know if I had a daughter.

GWEN: From the parallel world.

DIANE: That's not real.

GWEN: You're freaking out.

DIANE: Why are you telling me this?

GWEN: I have a picture.

> (*GWEN pulls a small photo from her pocket. Hands it to DIANE, who eyes it.*)

That's you. Holding me. When I was a baby.

DIANE: You could have faked this.

GWEN: I didn't.

DIANE: Do you want money? Is this a con?

GWEN: No! No. I just . . . I don't know. It's hard to know what to do. How to present this in a way that's not going to upset you, like you are now. Maybe this was a bad idea. Maybe I should have made my father do this. Because it's all his idea! But I wanted it too. Really badly.

DIANE: Wanted what?

GWEN: You to come back with us. I know! It's silly. But it's not. Because you're her. You're really her. And just now, I had a memory, of you bending over me in a park like this. I'm in a sandbox, and you're worried that I'm cold, you brought me a coat, it's pink. . . . I remember that coat. What you must think of me right now.

DIANE: I don't know what to think.

GWEN: I'm sorry. I am. But look at me. My face, my eyes. Do you see yourself in me, at all?

DIANE: I don't know.

GWEN: Do you want to?

DIANE: I don't know! If I believe this—and I'm not saying I do—then why didn't I meet your father in this world?

GWEN: I don't know.

DIANE: If he's my soulmate, if he's my destiny, shouldn't we have met?

GWEN: I guess it doesn't always work like that.

DIANE: Gwen—

GWEN: Do you believe that, if he's your soulmate, that you'll feel it immediately? That that will be enough?

DIANE: I do.

GWEN: Because he's here. My dad.

DIANE: What?

GWEN: Over there. Watching from behind the tree. I'm waving him over.

(GWEN waves.)

DIANE: Oh my goodness—

GWEN: No pressure. Forget I told you anything. Just meet my dad— his name is Jack—and see if you feel the spark. Even if it's just the seed of something, maybe you'll recognize it.

DIANE: The seed.

GWEN: Maybe you'll just know.

(JACK comes in. Very shy and nervous.)

Hey. She really isn't sure what to believe. But she wanted to meet you.

(DIANE looks at JACK. JACK looks at DIANE. Just staring.)

DIANE: Hi.

JACK: Hi.

(DIANE reaches out. Touches his face.)

This can't be real.

DIANE: That's supposed to be my line.

JACK: I never thought I'd see you again.

DIANE: I'm not her.

JACK: I know.

DIANE: But I guess I am, aren't I?

JACK: In all the best ways.

(DIANE touches his face again.)

DIANE: Can I bring my cats?

JACK: You can.

DIANE: Let's go.

(They all exit.)

END OF PLAY

THE SHAPE OF THE UNKNOWN

Emily McClain

Emily McClain is a professional playwright, theater educator, and a proud member of Working Title Playwrights and the Dramatists Guild. Her play *Slaying Holofernes* was cowinner of Essential Theatre's New Play Festival and received a world premiere production in 2019. Her full-length comedy *Julie's Place* was selected for the JOOKMS Spotlight Series in July 2020 and went on to be a semifinalist in the New American Voices Festival with The Landing Theatre Company. Her tragedy *Terminus Andronicus* was a 2019 finalist in the Shakespeare's New Contemporaries competition at the American Shakespeare Center. Her Risk Theatre play *Children of Combs and Watch Chains* was named a finalist for the Risk Theatre International Competition in August 2020 and was produced by the Quarantine Players in February 2021. She is published through ArtAge, Smith Scripts, and Stage-Write Plays, and more of her work can be found on the New Play Exchange (newplayexchange.org).

SYNOPSIS

Hank asks Laurel to join him for a night of romantic stargazing (she hopes!) and possible UFO sighting (he hopes!).

CHARACTERS

HANK, middle-aged, male, any race/ethnicity.
LAUREL, middle-aged, female, any race/ethnicity.

SETTING

An open field.

TIME

Near dusk.

NOTE

This play could be performed outside in a field at dusk. If outdoors, the audience should be seated on chairs or blankets spread out in a full circle around two lawn chairs.

MUFON is an acronym for Mutual UFO Network.

Two lawn chairs and blankets are set up about ten to fifteen feet apart from each other. HANK, a middle-aged man, is fiddling with the legs on a camera tripod standing by one of the lawn chairs as LAUREL, a middle-aged woman, brings a small cooler up from her car. She's wearing a camping headlamp.

HANK: Can you turn that off?

LAUREL: I didn't want to trip on something out here. It's getting hard to see.

HANK: Yeah, but the light . . . You need to give your eyes time to adjust as the sun is setting.

(LAUREL clicks the headlamp off, sighing irritably. HANK finishes setting up the camera tripod with the camera pointing high up above the horizon line. LAUREL sets the cooler down and then sits in her lawn chair.)

LAUREL: I brought beer. Want one?

HANK: No thanks. You shouldn't drink either. You don't want anything that might inhibit your powers of observation.

LAUREL: History says I can be plenty observant while drinking a beer. Several, in fact.

HANK: When we report what we see to MUFON, we have to indicate if either party was under the influence of drugs or alcohol at the time of the sighting. They don't come right out and SAY they disregard your sighting report if you have anything in that box on the form, but they might as well—

LAUREL: One beer isn't going to—

HANK: I don't want to risk it!

LAUREL: Fine.

(LAUREL takes the headlamp off, watching HANK, who is standing beside his lawn chair setup, scanning the sky.)

You gonna sit? Making me nervous.

HANK: Yeah, sorry.

(HANK sits in his chair with his gaze still upward.)

LAUREL: So . . . see anything?

HANK: Not yet. But it's still early.

LAUREL: Nice night, anyway.

HANK: Yes. It is.

LAUREL: Thanks for asking me to come out with you.

HANK: Sure. The MUFON people give more credence to your report if there are multiple witnesses.

LAUREL: Oh. Right. That makes sense.

HANK: Oh! I also, you know, wanted to spend time with—

LAUREL: No, yeah, it's fine. I wasn't thinking it was—

HANK: (*Overlapping.*) I mean, it's not like, a date or anything.

LAUREL: (*Overlapping.*) Obviously, this is not a date!

> (*They look at each other. Beat. They both look back up at the sky.*)

HANK: Right. So.

LAUREL: What makes you think we're facing the right direction, anyway?

HANK: Oh . . . I don't know. I just thought . . . No, you're absolutely right.

> (*HANK stands, picks up his lawn chair setup, and turns it to face the opposite direction. LAUREL stands to do the same.*)

No no no! You stay facing that way and I'll face this way, and that way no matter which way they come from, we'll be sure to see it.

LAUREL: Okay, sure. I'll face this way. Just . . . watching this direction.

HANK: So, couple of things.

LAUREL: Yeah?

HANK: Whatever we see we're probably not going to have a lot of time to observe, so we need to be prepared to take note of the major physical features: shape, estimated size, distance from us, texture, if we can make out any details like windows or engine mechanisms, whatever—

LAUREL: Okay . . .

HANK: On the MUFON form, the first major question is the shape of the object you see. You have to pick from a drop-down menu.

LAUREL: Really?

HANK: Yes. I'm going to read the list of options so you can have that fresh in your mind for when—

LAUREL: (*Overlapping.*) Uh, okay, I mean we might not even—

HANK: (*Overlapping.*) —for when you see something, you'll kind of already know the types of categories you're working with. Okay, ready?

    (*LAUREL nods.*)

Okay, so you've got, in alphabetical order: blimp, boomerang, bullet, cigar, cone, chevron, circle, cross, cylinder, diamond, disc, dumbbell, egg, fireball, flash, oval, Saturn-like, square/rectangular, star, teardrop, Tic Tac, triangle, other, unknown.

LAUREL: What the hell is Tic Tac-shaped?

HANK: You know . . . like, the candy?

LAUREL: Isn't that just a cylinder?

HANK: Well, no, I think a cylinder might have flat ends, and Tic Tac is more . . .

    (*He demonstrates with his hands. LAUREL scoffs.*)

LAUREL: Why don't they say pill-shaped? Or capsule? Seems more scientific than "Tic Tac."

HANK: I didn't make the list, I'm just sharing the—

LAUREL: (*Overlapping.*) And why are square/rectangle lumped together, but you've got circle, disc, and oval as three distinct categories?

HANK: Again, I didn't make the list.

LAUREL: I think it's odd that "unknown" is a choice. You're filling out this form because presumably you saw something, right? You wouldn't go to the trouble of doing it otherwise, so if you saw something you should be able to say a least the ballpark shape family, right?

HANK: I guess they want to leave room for people to admit that they couldn't be a hundred percent sure of what they saw, but they saw SOMETHING.

LAUREL: Hmm. I guess.

(Long beat of silence as they both stare in their opposite directions. LAUREL reaches her hand slowly down to the cooler beside her chair, ever so gently lifting the lid, trying to be as sneaky and silent as she can.)

HANK: (*Without breaking his gaze upward.*) No beer.

LAUREL: Fine! Jeez! (*Pause.*) Hank, this is so boring. What makes you think you're even gonna see anything out here anyway?

HANK: Just a feeling.

LAUREL: You seem mighty sure of this feeling. Drag out all this stuff in the middle of this field, buy that fancy tripod . . .

HANK: I've been needing a tripod for a few years anyway.

LAUREL: You really believe in this stuff? UFOs? Seriously, look at me.

(He does.)

I thought you were pulling my leg. Honestly, I thought it was an excuse to ask me out because you were shy or whatever—

HANK: Uh, okay, I mean, it's not a da—

LAUREL: (*Overlapping.*) Yes, you've mentioned! We're all very clear this is not a date!

HANK: Okay, sorry.

LAUREL: But I need you to, like, shoot straight with me here. Do you really, for real, believe that aliens are going to come to Earth tonight and YOU'RE going to be the one to see them?

HANK: No.

LAUREL: Oh! Okay, great.

HANK: I think WE'RE going to be the ones to see them.

LAUREL: Hank, no . . .

HANK: Why not? Why is that so crazy?

LAUREL: Because it's crazy! The fact that you have to even ask that question tells me that your grip on reality is a little questionable.

HANK: Well, my response to you is why is it so hard for you to believe? Look up, Laurel! There are millions upon millions upon MILLIONS of stars in our universe. That's ten followed by eighteen zeros worth of stars! Of that massive amount of stars, one star in a million has planets that orbit it like ours does. Of that smaller subset, one in a million has the right combination of physical factors to support planetary life as we know it.

LAUREL: Okay, so it's pretty damn unlikely then—

HANK: No! The opposite! That's one hundred million possible worlds where life could exist and evolve and where a species could reach the point of exploration beyond the bounds of their home galaxy. One hundred million opportunities for someone to reach out to this world!

LAUREL: I don't think that's the conclusion a logical person would draw from that data.

HANK: I disagree.

LAUREL: It's not an agree-to-disagree situation! You sound like a lunatic and you know it! What's driving all this? Are you really unhappy? Is this some kind of midlife crisis? Nervous breakdown? Low vitamin D? What's going on?

HANK: Can we just sit quietly? I don't want to get upset and risk missing something.

LAUREL: Fine.

> (*They both stare at the sky in malcontented silence. LAUREL glances over at HANK, but he stares resolutely at the sky, ignoring her. After a long period of silence:*)

Look, Hank, I'm sorry if what I said hurt your feelings.

HANK: (*Still looking skyward.*) It didn't.

LAUREL: I kinda think you might be lying to me.

HANK: (*Still looking skyward.*) I'm not.

LAUREL: Hank.

HANK: I'm not crazy.

LAUREL: Okay. That was harsh. You're right—

HANK: I dunno why I feel like I'm going to see something. I can't explain it. And I don't feel like I NEED to explain it.

LAUREL: It would help me understand this whole thing better. That's all.

> (*HANK continues to stare at the sky. LAUREL stares at him, hoping he will turn to look at her. He doesn't. She stands, putting her*

headlamp back on and gathering the cooler to leave. As she is taking a few steps to head back to her car, HANK speaks.)

HANK: When I look around at all the things that are wrong in this world, all the suffering, the cruelty, the unnecessary pain and needless misery. . . . It's so overwhelming. (*Pause.*) But then I think about those hundred million planets. The ones where life could have evolved? And I think that there's got to be, surely, out of those hundred million . . . at least a couple where they've managed to figure it out. I'd like to think so, anyway.

(LAUREL sets down the cooler and sits on it, listening. At some point in the following, HANK lowers his gaze to meet hers.)

This past year has been unimaginable. So much loss. I don't know of any group of people that wasn't touched by unexpected death in some way, you know? Folks said goodbye to loved ones over cell phones and computer screens. People went months without touching another human being. My father died in his nursing home, and the last time I spoke to him was through a glass window!

LAUREL: I know, Hank . . . I'm sorry.

HANK: That's not the— Look, it's not about that. It's about— Damn. I don't know. I just want an answer, Laurel. I want there to be an answer!

(HANK takes a moment to compose himself, then turns his attention back to the sky.)

So. I'm gonna sit here. And when they get here, I'm gonna ask them what the answer is.

(LAUREL watches him for a long moment. She stands and slowly returns to her lawn chair.)

LAUREL: Okay. Then I'm gonna sit here with you so you're not alone. (*Pause.*) My money's on egg shape. What do you think?

HANK: Yeah. Aerodynamic. Makes sense.

LAUREL: Yeah.

(She looks up at the sky. Silence.)

END OF PLAY

A SIGN IS A SIGN

Peter Dakutis

Peter Dakutis (he/him) lives in the Atlanta metro area and gets busy with his muse through playwriting. In addition to numerous local productions, his work has appeared around the United States and in London and Canada. His play *Transcodicil* was chosen for the Smith & Kraus *Best Ten-Minute Plays 2021* anthology. Peter is a member of the Atlanta Merely Writers playwriting group. He can be found on Facebook and at the New Play Exchange (newplayexchange.org).

SYNOPSIS

The sign says to wait until you are needed, but what if you're blocking someone else's way?

CHARACTERS

JOURNET, a person who is waiting to be needed. The character can be any age, gender, race, ethnicity, etc.

PORTER, a person who wants to get through a door that Journet is blocking. The character can be any age, gender, race, ethnicity, etc.

SETTING

An exterior door to a shop, office, or similar building.

TIME

The present.

JOURNET is standing patiently in front of the exterior door to a shop, office, or similar building. Next to JOURNET is a standing sign that says "Stand Here Until You Are Needed. Thank You." Under the wording is an arrow that points toward the door. PORTER enters, carrying a large and cumbersome potted houseplant or small tree. PORTER does not see the sign at first.

PORTER: Excuse me.

JOURNET: Yes?

PORTER: I'm going through that door. Could you move please?

JOURNET: Sorry, I can't.

PORTER: Why not?

JOURNET: The sign.

PORTER: What sign?

> *(JOURNET gestures to the sign. PORTER peers through the leaves of the plant to read it.)*

Oh. "Please stand here until you are needed." What does that mean?

JOURNET: It means I have to stand here until I am needed.

PORTER: Where did this sign come from? And why is it here?

JOURNET: I don't know.

PORTER: What do you mean you don't know?

JOURNET: I was feeling kind of depressed.

PORTER: So?

JOURNET: Well, it's a nice day, so I decided to go for a walk. Thought it might cheer me up. Then I saw the sign. So I'm waiting here.

PORTER: You have no idea who put it there or what it's for, but you're standing here waiting?

JOURNET: Yes.

PORTER: Why?

JOURNET: I think it's a sign.

PORTER: Of course, it's a sign. We've established that.

JOURNET: No, I mean a sign.

PORTER: Is there something wrong with you?

JOURNET: I mean a sign from God or the universe or whatever higher power you believe in.

PORTER: A sign from God?

JOURNET: Or the universe. Or the Flying Spaghetti Monster. Anything like that.

PORTER: Now I know there's something wrong with you. You look normal, but my father always said it's the normal-looking ones you have to watch out for.

JOURNET: You don't have to be rude.

PORTER: You're the one being rude. You're standing in front of the door and blocking me from entering.

JOURNET: The sign says to stand here.

PORTER: Could you just move a little to the left or the right? Or just step away so that I can get through?

JOURNET: The sign says to stand here. Not move around.

PORTER: And you're going to listen to that stupid sign, even though you know nothing about it?

JOURNET: Yes.

PORTER: Why? This is ridiculous.

JOURNET: I'm waiting to be needed.

PORTER: Needed for what?

JOURNET: I don't know. But I'm going to wait for it. No one needs me. All my life, I've never felt needed. My parents never said they needed me. None of my friends ever said they needed me. No one I've ever loved said they needed me. I certainly don't feel needed at work. I don't feel needed anywhere. By anybody. I'm just going through life without any purpose. Do you know what that's like?

PORTER: And you think you're going to find a purpose standing there? Just because of that stupid sign?

JOURNET: It's not a sign. It's a sign.

PORTER: You're an idiot.

JOURNET: Have you heard of the sickness unto death? Kierkegaard?

PORTER: No. It's not another coronavirus, is it? COVID-20? You're not contagious, are you? I can't deal with getting sick right now. Or dying, for that matter. Dying is not on my list of things to do today.

JOURNET: You're being overly dramatic.

PORTER: You're being overly stubborn. Is that part of your disease?

JOURNET: It's not a disease. The sickness unto death means I'm having an existential crisis.

PORTER: An existential crisis?

JOURNET: I call it the Batman of the soul.

PORTER: What does Batman have to do with any of this?

JOURNET: Batman, the Dark Knight?

PORTER: Now you've lost me.

JOURNET: The Dark Knight of the soul.

PORTER: My father warned me about people who idolize comic book characters.

JOURNET: Batman would understand.

PORTER: You are obviously having a nervous breakdown. And you're about to give me one. Are you homeless? My father always said to be careful around homeless people.

JOURNET: Your father seems awfully opinionated.

PORTER: You leave my father out of this.

JOURNET: You're the one who keeps bringing him up.

PORTER: What if I moved the sign to the side? Or kicked it over?

JOURNET: I'm staying in the spot the sign told me to.

PORTER: I'm trying to reason with you.

JOURNET: Kicking over a sign doesn't sound like reasoning to me.

PORTER: What if I give you some money to get out of the way?

JOURNET: I don't need money. I need to be needed. I believe in this sign, and I'm staying here until I'm needed.

PORTER: Why is this happening to me? Why today of all days? I can't deal with this. My life is spiraling out of control.

JOURNET: I'm sorry you're having a bad day.

PORTER: You're sorry I'm having a bad day? You're the one who's causing it.

JOURNET: I'm just following the sign.

PORTER: Okay, that's enough. This plant is heavy, and I'm tired of holding it. Take your Batman sickness and your neediness and whatever else is wrong with you and go somewhere else. Anywhere. I don't care.

JOURNET: I'm not doing it.

PORTER: I need you to get out of the way.

JOURNET: What?

PORTER: I need you to get out of the way.

JOURNET: You need me? Do you mean it?

PORTER: Yes, I mean it. I need you very much to let me go through that door.

JOURNET: You need me!

PORTER: Yes, I need you.

(JOURNET makes triumphant gestures.)

JOURNET: Yes! I knew if I waited long enough I would be needed.

(JOURNET steps forward slightly. With arms stretched and moving about, JOURNET tries to figure out how to hug PORTER.)

PORTER: What are you doing? Get out of my way.

JOURNET: I'm trying to give you a hug.

PORTER: If you touch me, I'll sue you for assault. Just go away.

(JOURNET steps back into their original spot.)

JOURNET: You lied to me. You don't need me.

PORTER: I ought to have you arrested. If I could dig out my phone, I'd call the police.

JOURNET: Go ahead. My life is meaningless anyway.

PORTER: I don't want to be mean. Please just move.

JOURNET: No. Standing here is the only thing that means anything to me right now.

PORTER: You know what? I'm done.

(*PORTER thrusts the plant at JOURNET, who takes it reluctantly.*)

You don't want to let me go in, you can take care of it.

(*PORTER exits. JOURNET looks around sheepishly.*)

JOURNET: Hello, plant. They weren't very nice, were they?

(*JOURNET starts to examine the plant.*)

You look kind of droopy. You haven't been watered in a while, and your foliage doesn't look good. All you need is a little love, don't you? I'm going to bring you home and take care of you.

(*Beat.*)

The sign was a sign, after all. (*À la Sally Field's Oscar acceptance speech.*) You need me. You really need me.

(*JOURNET exits.*)

END OF PLAY

STARMAN

Audrey Block

Audrey Block's work has appeared annually at the Fertile Ground Festival in Portland, Oregon. Her full-length play *Run of House* was a finalist for the 2021 Portland Civic Theatre Guild's New Play Award, and her ten-minute play *PDX* was honored by the Majestic Theatre in Corvallis, Oregon. She is a member of LineStorm Playwrights and the Dramatists Guild.

SYNOPSIS

An unexpected encounter in a Palm Desert, California, canyon unites two strangers in a moment, proving the power of being in the right place at the right time.

CHARACTERS

THE JUNIOR ASSOCIATE, late 20s, wearing clothes too trendy to be sold in stores.
HOOP GIRL, 40s, dressed in trending-on-Instagram dance wear.
TECHNICIAN, a voice counting up in the distance. Casting open.

SETTING

Night.

A desert enclave in Palm Desert, California. A sliver of moon dimly shining above red rocks.

The famous musician who lives here is hosting a party. Bursts of music come from his backyard and wind down the canyon like smoke. While partygoers mingle with friends, technicians prepare a space for the musicians to improvise outside.

We are in a circular space just above the party. It's the trailhead to the steep climb up the canyon. Tonight, the dirt here is raked smooth, and someone has created a glowing circle of fake-flickering, battery-operated candles. On the ground is a backpack, and beside it, a stack of LED hula hoops.

TIME

The present.

THE JUNIOR ASSOCIATE enters, using his phone as a flashlight. He walks to the edge of the glowing circle, stares at the mountains, and turns off the light.

THE JUNIOR ASSOCIATE: Hello?

(He checks the timer on his watch.)

Anyone here?

(He points his phone at the sky and waits for an app to identify the constellations. His phone chimes; his exact location is now saved to the cloud. In his hand is a live star map of the universe.)

HOOP GIRL: Behind you.

(He turns to see her, then turns back to studying the sky.)

THE JUNIOR ASSOCIATE: I didn't see you there.

HOOP GIRL: That was the point.

(THE JUNIOR ASSOCIATE watches the horizon, eyes adjusting to the angles of the jagged cliffs. HOOP GIRL moves a few steps closer to him.)

THE JUNIOR ASSOCIATE: This place is perfect.

HOOP GIRL: This place is reserved. Show me your wristband.

(Without looking away from the sky, he raises his left fist into the air. She points her flashlight at the lime-green beads knotted around his wrist.)

Which is it—Music Copyrights and Licensing or Bankruptcies and Dissolutions?

THE JUNIOR ASSOCIATE: Both. How'd you figure that out by looking at my bracelet?

HOOP GIRL: Green is code for newbie. And square beads mean you're either a lawyer or an accountant.

THE JUNIOR ASSOCIATE: Look, I get that I'm not the special guest that you were hoping for tonight. But all I need is . . . *(He checks his watch.)* . . . five minutes and fifty-six seconds of your time. And then I'll disappear.

HOOP GIRL: And what's happening in five minutes and . . .

(He checks his watch.)

THE JUNIOR ASSOCIATE: . . . forty-nine seconds? My brother is meeting me here. And he'll be easier to find in the dark.

(She moves closer to the edge of the circle, looking for a headlamp that is illuminating the trail. But there is only darkness. He walks to the opposite side of the circle, where the candles radiate a glow as soft and warm as the night air.)

It would help if you turned off the candles.

(She sizes him up, then walks to her backpack, pushes a button on a remote, and the candles turn off.)

Sometimes, on a clear night, I'll throw a blanket into my car and drive toward the desert. Other people like to go to the ocean, to listen to the waves. But I go to where the sky is filled with cosmic dust.

(He joins her, raising his phone to the sky.)

Have you ever used an app like this before?

HOOP GIRL: No. What's it do?

THE JUNIOR ASSOCIATE: It locates your place in the universe. And then it creates a star map of what's seeable. *(Pointing.)* There's Mars, and Rigel, and Arcturus. And here, where the mountain meets the horizon—that's where my brother will be.

HOOP GIRL: That's a dangerous trail to climb at night.

THE JUNIOR ASSOCIATE: My brother climbed Everest, twice. He'll be fine.

(His watch beeps, and he relaxes a little.)

So, what's on your agenda tonight?

HOOP GIRL: This is my retirement party.

THE JUNIOR ASSOCIATE: But you're not that old.

HOOP GIRL: Now you're being a kiss-ass. How would you know the shelf-life of a back-up singer and dancer?

(She walks to the pile of hoops, grabs one, tosses it into the air, and catches it.)

I'm not quitting everything. I'll still do the tribute band shows in Vegas. But not the world tours and the festivals. All that ended the night Beyoncé played Coachella. A revolution happened, and I watched it from the VIP tent.

THE JUNIOR ASSOCIATE: I was supposed to be there. But I got sent to Minneapolis to deal with the Prince clusterfuck.

(Music trails up the canyon. She presses a button on the hoop, and it fills with light. She steps into the hoop, raises it to her hips, and slowly it begins to whirl.)

HOOP GIRL: Tonight, I'm Hula Hoop Girl. Have you ever seen a hoop girl dance?

THE JUNIOR ASSOCIATE: Never on stage. They take up too much room, and they always screw up. Most insurance companies won't even cover hoop girls anymore.

(She stops spinning.)

HOOP GIRL: Careful. You don't want to be throwing shade at a host when your bracelet is that color. Greens are like pawns on a chessboard.

(She begins to spin again as the music shifts into a quiet, easy rhythm.)

Do you hear how he's asking me to join him? I can't describe how the connection is made. But what we do isn't a performance. It's part collaboration, part séance, part rebirth.

(She drops the hoop and switches to using it as a prop to stretch with.)

My first paid gig was as a hoop girl. I was at South by Southwest, dressed in a halter top and short shorts, and I was freezing. When I found a hoop on the ground, I started spinning to get warm. The band picked up the energy I was giving off and cleared a space for me beside the stage. At the end of the set, Mick Ralphs threw me a Bad Company T-shirt and a can of beer. And I became a dancer.

(*An alert on his phone.*)

But you don't roll like that, do you?

THE JUNIOR ASSOCIATE: You can't live in the moment when you bill by the hour.

(*His phone chimes.*)

Time to meet my brother.

(*He realigns the phone with the sky, launching the search. She turns the hoop off.*)

Do you see the three stars lined up like a triangle?

HOOP GIRL: Yes.

THE JUNIOR ASSOCIATE: Find those stars and follow them south, to the horizon.

(*The phone vibrates, and a new addition to the map appears—a white dot moving along a yellow arc.*)

HOOP GIRL: Why did a white dot just show up on the map? And why is it moving?

THE JUNIOR ASSOCIATE: That's the white dot you're going to find, using these.

(*He hands her a sleek set of binoculars. She points the binoculars at the sky, adjusting the focus. Suddenly, stars that were once hidden for millions of years wink.*)

HOOP GIRL: Who makes these? They're amazing.

THE JUNIOR ASSOCIATE: An optometrist sells them at Glastonbury.

HOOP GIRL: But you can't see anything at Glastonbury. It's always raining.

(His watch beeps, and a countdown begins. She scans the sky.)

What am I looking for?

THE JUNIOR ASSOCIATE: The same thing you see on my phone. A white dot moving east along the horizon.

(A long beep. A moment.)

He's here.

(She scans the sky with increasing agitation.)

HOOP GIRL: Where? I don't see him.

THE JUNIOR ASSOCIATE: You will.

(She tries again, lowers the binoculars, and takes a long step back. A pause.)

HOOP GIRL: So, I'm going to give you some time, alone, with your brother.

(She holds out the binoculars, but he doesn't take them.)

And when you're ready to say goodbye or goodnight—or whatever it is you say to each other—please, take the time you need to . . .

THE JUNIOR ASSOCIATE: *(He points.)* There he is.

(She looks up. The white dot is visible, even without binoculars.)

HOOP GIRL: That can't be an airplane. It's moving too fast.

(She focuses the binoculars on the dot.)

THE JUNIOR ASSOCIATE: It's the International Space Station. My brother lives there. He's an astronaut.

(He turns his phone's flashlight on, and the light begins to pulse in waves of color. He points the phone at the station and sends a text.)

HOOP GIRL: Can he see that?

THE JUNIOR ASSOCIATE: No. But I always send him a geotag of where we meet up. So he knows I was there.

HOOP GIRL: At the after-party for the Grammys, Jared Leto aimed a laser pointer at the moon, just because he wanted to beam some love there.

(A moment.)

Look at him go. How fast is he moving?

THE JUNIOR ASSOCIATE: Seventeen thousand, five hundred miles an hour. When he runs on the treadmill, he starts above Iceland and finishes above India.

(Flashes of light at the space station.)

HOOP GIRL: Why is it flashing like that?

THE JUNIOR ASSOCIATE: That's the sun, bouncing off the solar panels. He's close to the edge now. It's almost time for him to go.

HOOP GIRL: But he just got here.

(She lowers the binoculars. Together, they watch the sunlight strike the panels again and again. His watch beeps a final alert.)

THE JUNIOR ASSOCIATE: Later, bro.

(The white dot vanishes.)

You can turn the candles on now. He's gone.

(He accepts the binoculars from her. She turns the candles on and begins to move in preparation for her performance.)

HOOP GIRL: What does your brother do on the space station?

THE JUNIOR ASSOCIATE: Today he harvested a tray of radishes. If you follow his Twitter account, you'll learn that he's a fighter pilot who is fluent in Chinese and Russian. A colonel who teaches cyber warfare at the Naval Academy. Not the kind of guy you'd expect to shift from espionage to farming. All I know is that he orbits the Earth every ninety minutes—sixteen times a day—and most of the time, I forget that he's there.

HOOP GIRL: How far away do you think he is now?

THE JUNIOR ASSOCIATE: Light years ahead of me. My brother is like a machine that improves with every new demand you create for it. And me? I can amortize a thirty-year loan in my head. And I'm good at licensing Baby Yoda merch.

HOOP GIRL: Honestly, that sounds like more fun. When I imagine your brother's day, it's a list of things I hate: Filling out timesheets. Measuring what I eat. Being stuck in orbit instead of moving through the world, unleashed.

THE JUNIOR ASSOCIATE: If I sound envious, I'm not. It's like this whenever I see him. I enter a time machine and travel back to when I was the kid with a telescope at Space Camp. Then I flash forward ten years and remember what it felt like to pass out in the zero-gravity simulator. I washed out of the astronaut training program because I'm physically unable to survive in space.

And . . . I'm afraid of living in a box, floating beneath layers of hydrogen and helium. My brother thrives there.

(A beat.)

Do you know what I admire most about my brother? He's a zealot who circles the planet like a hawk. He doesn't stay awake at night thinking about the small dents in the seam of the ship that may be expanding. If it's a problem, NASA will add it to the inspection list.

(A TECHNICIAN begins a microphone check in the distance.)

TECHNICIAN: *(Off.)* Check one . . . two . . . three . . . four . . . Check one . . . two . . . three . . . four . . .

THE JUNIOR ASSOCIATE AND HOOP GIRL: *(Joining the count.)* Check one . . . two . . . three . . . four . . .

(The count stops.)

THE JUNIOR ASSOCIATE: How many people are you expecting here tonight?

HOOP GIRL: No one. Do you see that stack of hoops? Those are all for me. They're replacements for the ones that will bounce off the rocks and roll down the hill. If I were onstage tonight, you'd make it a drinking game. A shot of tequila every time a hoop drops.

(He looks at the blue dot atop the highest rock in the circle, where a tiny wireless camera is streaming live.)

THE JUNIOR ASSOCIATE: But there are cameras here, streaming your performance. Right?

HOOP GIRL: You're more like your brother than you realize. How many cameras do you count?

THE JUNIOR ASSOCIATE: Two, not including the drones. Will you send me the link, so I can watch?

HOOP GIRL: Beam me your contact info, and if I'm in the flow, I'll let you into the circle.

(Their phones confirm the exchange of information. Then, like a sprinter about to run a race, she shakes off the tension.)

Time for you to go. My friends are expecting me to light up the night and paint the air. And you've got dreams to hawk down there.

(A harmonica tunes, alongside a violin.)

You know what would make me happy tonight? The dumb joy of line dancing.

(She begins to move.)

Right, left, right. Grapevine. Kick. Turn. Right, left, right.

(He slips in beside her, as the warm-up music from the party boldens, and they let go, without inhibition. The music trails off, and the dancing stops.)

THE JUNIOR ASSOCIATE: And that's how I prove that I used to live in Texas.

(HOOP GIRL walks to her backpack and returns with a glow stick bracelet.)

HOOP GIRL: Take this with you.

(She breaks its seal and places it on his wrist.)

I always travel with them. They're better than nightlights for when you wake up in the dark and don't know where you are.

THE JUNIOR ASSOCIATE: Wish me luck.

HOOP GIRL: Luck burns out. Choose a star, and I'll wish on it.

(He looks at the sky.)

THE JUNIOR ASSOCIATE: It's hard to pick one.

HOOP GIRL: Then choose them all.

(He pauses, as if the moment were as solemn as prayer.)

THE JUNIOR ASSOCIATE: Done. You sure you want to be here, alone, dancing in the dark?

HOOP GIRL: Look around. Do you see all the lights glowing? That's the audience, marking their territory. When the music starts, no one here will be alone.

THE JUNIOR ASSOCIATE: Is that a line from a Coldplay song? Or does everything you say sound like song lyrics?

HOOP GIRL: Baby, it's all me.

THE JUNIOR ASSOCIATE: Well, figure out something useful I can offer in the future. Like tax advice. Or a Baby Yoda T-shirt. Because you're the oasis I just discovered in the desert.

(THE JUNIOR ASSOCIATE bows to her the way his favorite performer thanks an audience, and she answers with a flourish of her own. As he disappears into the dark, he sings the bridge to a chorus we all know—like Coldplay's "Viva La Vida"—and she answers as if they were friends who'd been saying goodbye to each other this way from the beginning.)

(A moment of silence, and then the famous musicians begin to play.)

END OF PLAY

STEPHANIE. FROM THE POSTERS.

Samantha Marchant

Samantha Marchant is a playwright and director based in Buffalo, New York. She graduated from Spalding University's MFA program in creative writing with a concentration in playwriting. Her work has been produced on both U.S. coasts and has had readings across the country and in Canada. Her plays have been produced or developed with The Workshop Theater's Intensive, The Skeleton Rep(resents), Theatre Three, TMDT, Post-Industrial Productions, Skull & Dagger, Alleyway Theatre, and Route 66, among others. Her writing has been published in *The Louisville Review*, *Sick Lit Magazine*, and *Women Writing Letters Season 3 and 4*. She is a Todd McNerney Playwriting Contest finalist, a B Street Theatre New Comedies Festival semifinalist, and a proud member of the Dramatists Guild, Queen City Playwrights, and BAWG Playwrights. She longs for what's weird and a good laugh. Find her plays on the New Play Exchange.

SYNOPSIS

Mike and Paul are both fathers of teenage girls. Paul wants to ask Mike if his daughter, Stephanie, can stay at Mike's house and hand out candy to trick-or-treaters with Mike's daughter and her friends, but something is holding him back. An examination of parenthood and how scary real life can be.

CHARACTERS

MIKE, Cori's dad.
PAUL, Stephanie's dad.

SETTING

Front stoop.

TIME

Halloween.

MIKE: Howdy.

PAUL: Oh.

MIKE: Hello.

PAUL: Is your wife at home?

MIKE: Is there something I can help you with?

PAUL: It's just . . . Cori said she was going to get her mom.

MIKE: Her mom stepped out.

PAUL: Will your wife be back soon?

MIKE: I don't know.

PAUL: Ballpark time frame?

MIKE: She's out getting more candy. You know how stores are on Halloween.

PAUL: So . . . around . . . when?

MIKE: I don't know. Could be soon.

PAUL: Oh. Good.

MIKE: Could be hours.

PAUL: Oh.

MIKE: Do you know my wife?

PAUL: I'm Stephanie's dad.

MIKE: I'm Mike. Cori's dad.

PAUL: Paul. *Stephanie's* dad.

MIKE: Right.

PAUL: Do you remember Stephanie?

MIKE: Stephanie . . . ? Sure.

PAUL: Stephanie is hoping to stay and hand out candy with Cori and her friends.

MIKE: Sure.

PAUL: I was hoping to touch base with Cori's mom . . .

MIKE: I'm Cori's dad.

PAUL: You know . . . because Stephanie and I were out walking . . .

MIKE: Trick-or-treating.

PAUL: She doesn't want me to call it that.

MIKE: Sure.

PAUL: And we got to your house and saw the kids, and Stephanie asked to stay and hand out candy . . . and I wanted to be able to say,

"Yes," but . . . you know. . . . So, I asked Cori if I could speak to her mom on account of . . . you know. And not to be a burden, but . . .

MIKE: I've got half Cori's class out on my lawn. I can watch another one, no problem.

PAUL: But . . .

MIKE: What?

PAUL: Nothing.

MIKE: What is it?

PAUL: You're not really watching them though, are you?

MIKE: Sure I am.

PAUL: From inside.

MIKE: They're fifteen.

PAUL: Exactly.

MIKE: They can function on their own.

PAUL: I know.

MIKE: Then what's up your ass?

PAUL: Excuse me?

MIKE: You're acting like it's a crime that I'm choosing not to leer at a bunch of fifteen-year-old girls.

PAUL: Watching them isn't leering.

MIKE: Looking at teenage girls is always leering. That's why I watch them from inside where I can't see them.

PAUL: That's ridiculous.

MIKE: Look, if something happens, they'll come get me.

PAUL: What if they don't?

MIKE: If something really bad happens . . .

PAUL: How can you predict what a teenager is going to do?

MIKE: You can't.

PAUL: And that doesn't scare you?

MIKE: Of course it does. But what are you going to do?

PAUL: Watch them.

MIKE: Forever? Hold on. Are they talking about condoms again?

   (To unseen kids.)

Sweetie? Remember you're allergic to latex?

   (Watching the kids but speaking to PAUL.)

And . . . they're taunting her. My kid's never going to have sex. Swoop in and out. Squash the big issues. Let them figure out the rest. That's called parenting.

PAUL: Hardly.

MIKE: What would you do?

PAUL: I would go over there . . .

MIKE: Whoa, whoa, whoa, you can't go over there.

PAUL: Why not?

MIKE: That's a pack of teenage girls.

PAUL: And I'm an adult.

MIKE: They're mean.

PAUL: Are you scared of a bunch of kids?

MIKE: Sure. Aren't you?

PAUL: I'm scared for them.

MIKE: Life's going to happen.

PAUL: Shouldn't we at least try to protect them?

MIKE: I'm just inside.

PAUL: You're the dad.

MIKE: What's the worst that could happen?

PAUL: You're asking me that?

MIKE: Yeah. Seems you've got an overactive imagination. They're a bunch of kids looking after one another. And if blood or other bodily fluids come on the scene, they'll come get me.

PAUL: But, what if . . .

MIKE: What if they eat too much candy? What if the house gets egged? What if a glittery vampire shows up, and they start having an orgy?

PAUL: This is why I wanted to talk to your wife.

MIKE: That's bullshit.

PAUL: Excuse me?

MIKE: Moms are not automatically better than dads.

PAUL: I'm a dad, too.

MIKE: And you think you're better than me.

PAUL: Hey . . .

MIKE: Leave your kid here or not. I don't need any more crap.

PAUL: You know . . . it's probably best if Stephanie and I go.

MIKE: Go.

(*Pointing at PAUL.*)

There goes Dad of the Year, over here. He's there with the Band-Aid before the blood spills.

PAUL: Listen, pal.

MIKE: Make me.

PAUL: It's becoming clear that you don't really remember who Stephanie is.

MIKE: She's some kid in Cori's class.

PAUL: No. She's not. Not anymore. She's been homeschooled since second grade.

MIKE: Oh, get off your homeschooled high horse.

PAUL: You don't understand the situation.

MIKE: Why should I remember Stephanie if she's been too good for public school?

PAUL: I respect the public school system. They were very supportive two months back with our search. Maybe you saw the poster they sent home with Cori?

MIKE: Of the missing kid. Sure. They were plastered all over town. The kid turned up though. All a misunderstanding. Shit. *Stephanie.* From the posters.

PAUL: Yeah.

MIKE: I'm glad she's back home. Safe.

PAUL: Thank you.

MIKE: Do you know what went on while . . . ?

PAUL: No.

MIKE: Did you ask her?

PAUL: Of course not.

MIKE: You gonna handcuff yourself to her for the rest of your life?

PAUL: My sister flew in. She and I are tag-teaming it.

MIKE: Sure.

PAUL: Tonight's my first shift on my own.

MIKE: Halloween. A doozy. When things go bump in the night.

PAUL: When Stephanie was missing, I prayed. I hadn't prayed since I was a little kid, but then I was praying day and night. Praying that she was getting food and had a place to sleep. And that whoever took her wasn't. . . . That she still had all her fingers and toes. I prayed that whatever sick monster took her would get what was coming to him.

MIKE: Sure.

PAUL: A monster. That's who I thought took Stephanie. When I spent all that time praying. What I pictured in my mind wasn't a man. But an actual monster. I thought Stephanie was in an absolute real, horrifying situation, but all I could picture was a cartoonish imp with a hunched back and jagged claws.

MIKE: . . . Yeah.

PAUL: I'm the monster.

MIKE: No . . .

PAUL: Then who is? Nobody took her. She ran away. Is Stephanie the monster?

MIKE: No.

PAUL: Of course not. She's just a girl who is so unhappy that she decides her only option is to run away. No one took her. And she's not the monster. So that leaves me. The man she ran away from.

MIKE: That's not fair.

PAUL: When she came to live with me after her mom died . . . I told myself I was going to be the "Cool Dad," you know? I don't think I can pull that off, can I?

MIKE: That ship has sailed. "Cool Dad" is a myth anyway.

PAUL: I don't know if I can do this.

MIKE: You are, though . . . doing it.

PAUL: My sister's eventually going to fly home. And then it'll be back to just me and Stephanie. What am I supposed to do? I just want to give her what she needs, but that obviously isn't good enough, you know? How am I supposed to know what she . . . ? Her mom told me I wasn't cut out for this. But she's dead now and there's nothing she can do. . . . This is why you write a will. God. I need to write a will.

MIKE: Maybe you should talk to my wife.

PAUL: I shouldn't be unloading this on you.

MIKE: My wife, she's a lawyer. She could help you out with that will. And she is better than me. At some things. She could give you some tips on parenting teenage girls.

PAUL: Thanks.

MIKE: But what I said is true. Not all moms are automatically better than dads. We've all got our issues. And we all have our strengths. We all just need to keep . . . trying.

PAUL: Watching her forever isn't the best solution, is it?

MIKE: Try talking to her sometime.

PAUL: I'm scared. What is she going to say?

MIKE: I don't know.

PAUL: . . . Why? You know?

    (Beat.)

I will. Ask her. Talk to her. Eventually. Is it OK if I watch for a bit longer?

MIKE: Sure.

END OF PLAY

TALE OF A GIRL
A Short Musical
Holly Yurth Richards

Holly Yurth Richards is an award-winning playwright, composer, lyricist, novelist, and poet. She holds a degree in interdisciplinary studies, focusing on writing, story theory, and music theory. Holly is a member of LineStorm Playwrights, Maestra Music, the Dramatists Guild, and the American Society of Composers, Authors and Publishers (ASCAP), and was recently appointed to the grants review panel for the National Endowment for the Arts Theater and Musical Theater team. Holly and her husband, Derek, run their own publishing company, Octavo Publishing, LLC, and write books together and independently. Holly lives in Tualatin, Oregon, with her husband and their blended family of eight amazing children and zero pets.

SYNOPSIS

The Wind brings Girl into the world and has a hard time sharing her with Boy.

CHARACTERS

PLAYER 1, storyteller, any gender, higher voice.
PLAYER 2, storyteller, any gender, lower voice.
GIRL, late teens, lyrical and fiery.
BOY, late teens or early 20s, charismatic and strong.
WIND, ageless, female persona who can be played by any gender,
    comedic and ridiculous.

SETTING

Somewhere in the countryside near the sea.

TIME

Long ago.

In the countryside, close to the sea. Long ago.

PLAYER 1: We are about to hear a story—

PLAYER 2: —watch a story—

PLAYER 1: —feel a story—

PLAYER 1 AND 2: —from long ago.

PLAYER 1: And if you listen closely enough—

PLAYER 2: —watch closely—

PLAYER 1 AND 2: —you might not miss it.

    (WIND enters, full of exaggerated movement and attempted grace.)

PLAYER 1:
        ONCE, IN A TOWN
        CLOSE BY THE SEA

> THE WIND SPOKE UP
> MADE HER WISHES KNOWN

PLAYER 2:

> CAME RUSHING THROUGH
> THE FALLING LEAVES

PLAYER 1 AND 2:

> AND ON HER BREATH
> INTO THE WORLD WAS BLOWN
> OO—
> A LITTLE GIRL

(GIRL, late teens/early adulthood, seems to emerge from nothing.)

PLAYER 1: She had no sister.

PLAYER 2: She had no brother.

PLAYER 1: No mother—

(WIND gives a disapproving look toward PLAYER 1.)

PLAYER 2: —or father—

PLAYER 1: —she came into the world alone.

PLAYER 1 AND 2: But she was—

PLAYER 1 AND 2:

> FULL OF FIRE
> LIKE NO OTHER
> IN THE WORLD

PLAYER 1:

> AND THE WIND DID BRAID HER HAIR

(WIND rustles through her curls.)

PLAYER 2:

> AND THE SEA GAVE HER SALMON AND
> PEARLS

PLAYER 1 AND 2:

> AND THE FIRE IN HER BONES
> KEPT HER WARM
> AS A WOMAN UNFURLED

(GIRL begins to dance with WIND, interacting with the PLAYERS.)

WIND:

> HUSH, MY DEAR DAUGHTER
> DON'T YOU CRY
> IF ANYONE TRIES TO TAKE YOU
> *(Suddenly menacing.)*
> THEY'LL DIE

PLAYER 1: She might not have gone to school or church—

PLAYER 2: —but she knew the truth—

PLAYER 1: —and she knew her worth.

PLAYER 2: She had all that she needed—

PLAYER 1: —and she wanted what she had . . .

(BOY enters. He is handsome and strong. GIRL leaps back to observe from a distance.)

PLAYER 1:

> 'TIL A BOY WALKED BY ONE DAY

PLAYER 2: He didn't talk to the girl . . .

PLAYER 1 AND 2:

> NOT THAT SHE WOULD WANT HIM TO,
> ANYWAY

PLAYER 1: —but she did want it.

PLAYER 1 AND 2: She wanted it more than anything in the world.

(BOY sees GIRL and is startled.)

BOY:

WHO ARE YOU?

GIRL:

WHO ARE YOU?

BOY: I'm sorry . . .

I'M JUST NOT USED TO SEEING ANYONE
WHEN I WALK THIS WAY

GIRL:

WHEN YOU WALK THIS WAY?

BOY: Yes!

ESPECIALLY NOT A GIRL

GIRL: —a girl?

BOY: Yes. A girl.

GIRL: *(Touching her throat, top of her chest.)*

GIRL . . .

And you?

BOY: *(Touching his chest.)* A boy.

GIRL: *(Reaching out for him.)*

BOY . . .

(WIND's eyes begin to grow wild watching the two.)

PLAYER 2: The boy was drawn to the girl like she was his destination
all along.

(BOY and GIRL dance and then settle into each other for the night, as WIND grows increasingly fierce.)

PLAYER 1:

>AND THE WIND DID PUFF HER CHEST

PLAYER 2:

>SHE WAS JEALOUS AND FITFUL WITH FEAR

PLAYER 1 AND 2:

>SHE ROSE UP
>AND WHILE THEY SLEPT
>MADE THE BOY DISAPPEAR

(There is a flash of light. BOY seems to disappear into nothing. GIRL sits up and smiles.)

PLAYER 1: When the girl rose the next morning, she was alone.

PLAYER 2: She didn't remember the boy.

PLAYER 1:

>FOR THE WIND HAD BLOWN SO FIERCELY
>THE WORLD STOPPED IN ITS TRACKS

PLAYER 2:

>THE WORLD STOPPED IN ITS TRACKS

PLAYER 1 AND 2:

>STOPPED TURNING ON ITS AXIS

PLAYER 1:

>THEN STARTED SPINNING BACK

PLAYER 2:

>THEN STARTED SPINNING BACK
>BACK THROUGH THE NIGHT

PLAYER 1 AND 2:

>TO THE DAY BEFORE

PLAYER 1:

        AND THE BOY WAS NO MORE

(WIND pushes GIRL along, taking her to a new place. Along the way, WIND produces random treasures to keep GIRL occupied, whispering in her ear to teach her the right words as they go.)

PLAYER 1: It wasn't hard to divert her attention, for she didn't remember him, after all.

PLAYER 2: And the wind would do anything to keep it that way.

GIRL: *(Receiving or pointing out each item, listening, then repeating.)*
        SHELL
        BUTTERFLY
        SNAKE

(GIRL startles and drops it.)

Oh! No.

        MOSS AND FERNS
        BIRD
        BUTTERFLY
        BOY

WIND: What?

(GIRL is looking far off.)

PLAYER 2:

        'TIL A BOY WALKED BY ONE DAY

(BOY enters. He is handsome and strong. GIRL leaps back to observe from a distance.)

PLAYER 2: He didn't talk to the girl—

PLAYER 1 AND 2:

        NOT THAT SHE WOULD WANT HIM TO,
        ANYWAY

PLAYER 1: —But she did want it.

PLAYER 1 AND 2: She wanted it more—

WIND: —Okay, that's *enough.*

PLAYER 1:
> AND THE WIND
> IT STARTED TO BLOW

(BOY and GIRL wrap their arms around each other.)

GIRL: Hold on!

BOY: I'm holding!

PLAYER 2:
> TIME STARTED TO SLOW

PLAYER 1 AND 2:
> TO GO IN REVERSE

PLAYER 1: And before the wind knew what she was doing—

PLAYER 1 AND 2:
> SHE HAD SENT THEM BOTH
> TO THE UNKNOWN UNIVERSE

WIND: Damn it.

(Beat. WIND signals to the PLAYERS to start things over again.)

PLAYER 1:
> ONCE, IN A TOWN
> CLOSE BY THE SEA
> THE—

WIND: Blah, blah—we know the thing. Poof! I made a girl.

(GIRL seems to emerge from nothing.)

PLAYER 1 AND 2:

OO—

A LITTLE GIRL

PLAYER 1: No matter how many times the wind tried to keep the boy at bay—

PLAYER 1 AND 2: —He would always come—

PLAYER 2: —and they would always fall in love.

PLAYER 1:

SO, WITH DEFEATED BREATH

THE WIND LEFT WITH A SIGH

PLAYER 1 AND 2:

AAH

PLAYER 2:

THE GIRL BARELY NOTICED

AS THE CALM DAYS ROLLED BY

PLAYER 1:

THE FALL BECAME WINTER

THE WINTER BECAME SPRING

PLAYER 2:

AND AS THE SUN GREW WARMER

PLAYER 1:

DAYS GREW LONGER

PLAYER 1 AND 2:

SHE FOUND HERSELF WISHING

PLAYER 1:

FOR A BREEZE

PLAYER 2: And so the girl found the longest rope that she could.

PLAYER 1: The boy lassoed one end to the sun—

PLAYER 2: —and the other to the moon—

PLAYER 1: —and the rope played red rover with the earth.
FOR THE GIRL HELD ON SO FIERCELY
THE WORLD STOPPED IN ITS TRACKS

PLAYER 2:
THE WORLD STOPPED IN ITS TRACKS

PLAYER 1 AND 2:
STOPPED TURNING ON ITS AXIS

PLAYER 1:
THEN STARTED SPINNING BACK

PLAYER 2:
THEN STARTED SPINNING BACK
BACK THROUGH THE DAYS

PLAYER 1 AND 2:
TO THE AUTUMN BEFORE

PLAYER 1:
AND THE CALM WAS NO MORE . . .

(WIND comes back on the scene in glorious, comedic, powerful gusts. GIRL stops the show.)

GIRL: Wait, wait—all we needed was a breeze. I didn't ask for all of this blustery nonsense!

WIND: Look, missy—if you want me back, you have to want all of me, okay? This is how I am sometimes. Like, me and the Pacific Ocean just broke up, because they were all, "You bring too many hurricanes into my life, and then all the people start being sick of me and then they want to kill the dolphins and stuff, and, like, oh my God, you're so dramatic," and I was like, "Whatever, this is what I was meant to do, okay, and I won't be with someone who keeps me from realizing my full potential," and they were all, "You suck," and I was like, "No—I don't, I blow—which totally goes to show that—just like I thought—you were never really seeing me anyway, so fine, screw you," and they were all, "Yeah, because you're invisible," and I went ripping out of there, and I promised myself I would never, *ever* allow myself to be stifled again!

(*Beat.*)

GIRL: Maybe we could compromise?

WIND: (*Considers.*) Will you still let me braid your hair?

(*GIRL turns around to give WIND access to her hair.*)

WIND: (*Still considering, looking at BOY.*) Does he have to stay around?

GIRL: Well, don't you want me to be happy?

WIND: (*Hopeful.*) You really wanted me back?

GIRL: (*Turning to give WIND an embrace.*) Really, truly.

BOY: She did.

WIND: (*Hissing through her teeth.*) I'm not asking you!

(*To GIRL.*) Have you been eating? Did you find the fig bar I left you? Is he treating you nice? Do you have good boundaries in place?

(*As the PLAYERS begin to sing, GIRL insists on WIND dancing with BOY. At first, WIND acts disgusted, but BOY sweeps her off her feet. By the last note, WIND is wrapped up in his arms as GIRL laughs.*)

PLAYER 1:

>> ONCE, IN A TOWN
>> CLOSE BY THE SEA

> THE WIND SPOKE UP
> MADE HER WISHES KNOWN

PLAYER 2:

> CAME RUSHING THROUGH
> THE FALLING LEAVES

PLAYER 1 AND 2:

> AND ON HER BREATH
> INTO THE WORLD WAS BLOWN
> OO—
> A LITTLE GIRL

END OF PLAY

Tale of a Girl

music, lyrics, and book by
Holly Yurth Richards

P1: We are about to hear a story -
P2: - watch a story -
P1: - feel a story -
P1 & 2: - from long ago...

P1: And if you listen closely enough -
P2: - watch closely -
P1 & 2: - you might not miss it.

Once, in a town close by the sea, the wind spoke up, made her

P1: wish-es known... and on her breath, in - to the

P2: Came rush-ing through the fall-ing leaves, and on her breath, in - to the

Girl: A girl?
Boy: Yes, a girl.

Girl...

Girl: And you?
Boy: - a boy.

Boy...............

girl

P2: The boy was drawn to the girl
like she was his destination all along.

And the   wind   did puff   her

chest.

She was   jea - lous and   fit - ful with   fear.

Once, in a town close by the sea, the

wind spoke up, made her wish-es known... and

Came rush-ing through the fall-ing leaves, and

on her breath, in – to the world was blown Oo_____ a lit-tle girl.

on her breath, in – to the world was blown Oo_____ a lit-tle girl.

THE THING ABOUT LIGHTHOUSES
A Monologue . . . Sort Of

Josie Seid

Josie Seid currently lives in Portland, Oregon, and is a proud member of LineStorm Playwrights. She is the author of *Petite Dames*, which was nominated for The Kilroys List in 2015 and workshopped at Lewis & Clark's Ray Warren Symposium on Race and Revolutionary Struggle. Other works include: *Fezziwig's Fortune*, *Path of Glory*, *The Great God of the Dark Storm Cloud*, *Jordan's Wisdom*, *Overdue*, *Stand by Me*, and *This Is Message Number 13*. As a writer, she approaches stories with a multifaceted lens due to the privilege of assuming many different hats in the world of theater. At one time or another she has been an actor, director, or costumer for the stage. She states: "In my writing, I try to be or represent the 'other voice' to share that view or story that gets brushed under the rug; for if we cannot use our gifts to make the world a little clearer, a little more understanding, a little more human, why are we doing this work?"

SYNOPSIS

Ravyn reflects on a series of events surrounding her missing father. A most unexpected source assists in achieving resolution within her fractured family dynamics.

CHARACTERS

RAVYN, female, 18+, African American.
GHOST, female, 25+, any race.

SETTING

A lighthouse.

TIME

Current.

NOTE

If the piece is performed as a monologue, the voice of the ghost can be prerecorded or can be sung by the actor playing Ravyn.

The song is in the tune of "Wayfaring Stranger," which is public domain.

RAVYN: "Did you know that there are over 700 working lighthouses in the U.S., and of those 700, 115 are in the state of Michigan? Fascinating!" my mother said. "Now, the thing about lighthouses is that they elicit a very specific feeling in people. Everyone has a reaction to the thought of lighthouses—they're beautiful, they're majestic, they're lonely . . ."

I found them creepy as all get out. They always felt to me as if they were waiting for someone who didn't really care about them. Standing sentinel in a one-way love affair. Little did I know, I was closer to the reason for my mom's newfound fascination with lighthouses than I realized.

To give you some background, by the time we were having this conversation, I was the eldest of three children with my mom being a single parent. We'll get to that in a moment. We were all girls, me at thirteen, and my two twin sisters were ten. Now I say my mom was a single parent, but that was not fully true. See, my dad was a merchant mariner, and he was gone a lot. I mean *a lot* a lot. The last time I saw him was just after the twins were born, and by now, I was feeling pretty sure he wasn't coming back. My mom, on the other hand, loved him deeply and actively. She never gave up on him.

Which leads us to the lighthouse. My mother's new fascination with lighthouses was much more than that. It was an introduction to what was to be our new home. She had signed up to be a keeper for a lighthouse in Michigan. It was no mistake that the lighthouse was close to the base that my dad had associated with and was the last place he shipped out of before his disappearance from our family. So, Ohio to Michigan as the crow flies, and we were all packed up and settled in within a month.

It didn't take long after that for things to get weird.

Lighthouses come in many shapes and sizes; this one was designed so that the tower was actually connected to the house. The house was old, and creaky, and drafty . . . and haunted. My mom denied it, but she had to stop denying it when the ghost started not only singing with her but changing her song. See, when my mom got spooked or sad or even frustrated, she would sing. I didn't learn about the spooked part until we moved into the lighthouse, to be fair. This is how it went. As I mentioned, the tower of the lighthouse was connected to our house. On the back of the house were stairs that led right down to the beach. That would have been cool but for the fact that this water was always frigid, and the wind seemed to always be whistling, and it was worse at night. My mom's job was essentially to keep the light burning, and she would check on it every night at about 2:00 a.m. After the first two trips up there the week we arrived, she started singing.

(Sings.)

> I'M JUST A POOR WAYFARING STRANGER,
> TRAVELING THROUGH THIS WORLD OF WOE
> BUT THERE'S NO SICKNESS, TOIL OR DANGER
> IN THAT LAND TO WHICH I GO—

It was haunting, but beautiful too. I admit, I always loved my mom's singing. . . . Then, I heard it, and I know my mom did too . . .

GHOST: (*Sings.*)

> I'M GOING THERE TO MEET MY LOVER
> I KNOW HE'LL GREET ME WHEN I COME
> I'M ONLY GOING O'ER THE WATER
> FOLLOW MY LIGHT AND RETURN HOME

RAVYN: Like I said. Creepy. For about a month after that, my mom cut out the singing. But that other voice didn't stop. She'd sing the song every night at 2:00 when my mom went up to check the light. It went on that way for a while. Several months. Then the weirdest thing yet happened. One night at 2:00 a.m. on the dot, the singing started. It was different this time.

GHOST: (*Sings.*)

> NO MORE I FEAR SHADOW OR DARKNESS
> FOR I HAVE KNOWN A DEEPER WOE
> AND YET I STAND WITH HIGH-HELD LANTERN
> AND PRAYERS THIS LIGHT WILL LEAD YOU
> HOME

RAVYN: My mom was there, frozen. A tear came to her eye, and she joined in—

(*Sings.*)

> I'M GOING THERE TO MEET MY LOVER
> I KNOW HE'LL GREET ME WHEN I COME
> I'M ONLY GOING O'ER THE WATER
> FOLLOW MY LIGHT AND RETURN HOME

The tower lit up like it was on fire, but we knew it wasn't, because the light was somehow cold. Blue. That light dimmed slightly and came floating across the balcony that encircled the tower, down the steps to the beach, and out to sea. We thought we had seen the end of the ghost. But then—a light in the distance and the first boat we had seen since we'd been here. It wasn't a ship. It was a small boat, like a rescue craft. We all stood there, eyes glued to the dot on the waves as it came in closer and closer and closer. Then, my mom let out a scream—surprise mixed with disbelief.

I kid you not, it was my dad. Back. Exhausted. Emaciated. But alive. My mother ran into the water, and with a strength I didn't know she had, she dragged that boat up onto the beach, and she and my dad stood embracing. Motionless. They looked like statues with a weird blue glow from the moonlight illuminating their figures. On the water, we heard that song come back to us:

GHOST: (*Sings.*)

> NO MORE I FEAR, SHADOW OR DARKNESS
> FOR DEAR, MY WILL HAS BROUGHT YOU HOME
> WHILE HERE I STOOD, WITH HIGH-HELD LANTERN
> YOU SAW MY LIGHT AND FOLLOWED ON
> MY ARMS EMBRACE YOU, OH, MY LOVER
> AND NEVER MORE WILL LET YOU GO
> MY SOUL HAS FOUND
> THE REST I SOUGHT FOR
> NO MORE I'LL WEEP
> NO MORE I'LL MOAN.

END OF PLAY

THE TOTAL SPIRITUAL

Rich Orloff

Rich Orloff writes plays in a myriad of styles and settings. His short comedy *The Total Spiritual* is part of his short play collections *Take It Outside!* (nine short plays set outdoors) and *Pool Party* (nine short plays set around and in a pool). The *New York Times* called his play *Big Boys* "rip-roaringly funny" and named *Funny as a Crutch* a Critic's Pick. Rich's comedy *Romantic Fools* has had more than one hundred productions around the world, including two in Madrid, where apparently, they're no better at romance than we are. Rich has written more than eighty short plays, which have had more than two thousand productions on six of the seven continents—and a staged reading in Antarctica. Seven have been included in Applause Books' annual *Best American Short Plays* anthology, and five have been published in *Best Ten-Minute Plays*. He likes the sound of laughter. Website: richorloff.com.

SYNOPSIS

A very confused and newly deceased person finds that the entrance exam to the Hereafter is filled with trick questions.

CHARACTERS

THE INTERVIEWER, any age or gender.
THE APPLICANT, any age or gender.
Member(s) of THE BUCKET BRIGADE, any age or gender. (This can be one person, or someone different with each entrance.)

SETTING

Above and beyond.

TIME

The present.

NOTE

A simple set: a table or desk, a couple of chairs, and a pool. (Of course, the pool doesn't have to be literal. That's the magic of theater.)

As the play begins, the INTERVIEWER is making notes at a desk. A member of the BUCKET BRIGADE enters, carrying a large bucket of water.

INTERVIEWER: Need any help?

BUCKET BRIGADE: No, I got it.

INTERVIEWER: Looks like a heavy one.

BUCKET BRIGADE: Yeah, well, there's been a slew of people hearing bad medical news, and a couple of natural disasters, and a lot of people touched by unexpected acts of kindness.

(The BUCKET BRIGADE pours the bucket into the pool. The pool glistens.)

INTERVIEWER: Send the next one in, okay?

BUCKET BRIGADE: Will do.

(The BUCKET BRIGADE exits. A moment later, the APPLICANT enters.)

INTERVIEWER: Have a seat.

APPLICANT: Wow, this is, this is—I didn't expect it to be so—

INTERVIEWER: I know. It's a big adjustment. Have a seat.

APPLICANT: I mean, it's not every day—

INTERVIEWER: Relax. Breathe. And have a seat.

APPLICANT: Are, uh, are you—

INTERVIEWER: I just help out.

APPLICANT: How long have you been helping out?

INTERVIEWER: Not long. About eight hundred years.

APPLICANT: Wow.

INTERVIEWER: I'm one of the new kids. So . . . how was the funeral?

APPLICANT: It was, it was—good, I guess. Huge turnout.

INTERVIEWER: I'm glad.

APPLICANT: I was amazed at some of the things people said. I never realized people liked me so much.

INTERVIEWER: I know. Sometimes I think we'd enjoy funerals more if we had them *before* we dropped dead. Now then, about your life—

APPLICANT: I know I made a lot of mistakes. I was selfish, and I coveted a few things I should've never coveted—

INTERVIEWER: Relax.

APPLICANT: I know it's late, but I swear I'm willing to atone for anything and everything—

INTERVIEWER: If people were angels when alive, then heaven would be a rerun.

APPLICANT: It's just, if I could only—

INTERVIEWER: Relax. We have all the time in the world.

APPLICANT: I just—

INTERVIEWER: One of the best parts of heaven is that nobody's in a hurry.

APPLICANT: Really?

INTERVIEWER: It changes the quality of supermarket lines considerably.

APPLICANT: There are supermarkets in heaven?

INTERVIEWER: And they're never out of stock.

APPLICANT: Wow.

INTERVIEWER: Clothing stores always have your size. And you can return things without a receipt.

APPLICANT: So, so you mean, like, you don't just lie around on clouds all day and strum harps?

INTERVIEWER: I'd rather go to hell. No, we have the complete range of activities here: golf, bowling, karaoke.

APPLICANT: Karaoke?

INTERVIEWER: Nobody's forced to go.

APPLICANT: Wow.

INTERVIEWER: Heaven is simply life without the stress.

APPLICANT: Sign me up.

INTERVIEWER: Welllllllllllllll . . .

APPLICANT: Uh-oh.

INTERVIEWER: It's not like that.

APPLICANT: I really planned to pay that money back.

INTERVIEWER: You should've lived so long.

(A member of the BUCKET BRIGADE enters, carrying a bucket.)

BUCKET BRIGADE: Coming through.

INTERVIEWER: Looks pretty full.

BUCKET BRIGADE: A whole bunch of people just fell in love, there was a new outbreak of violence somewhere, and a bunch of five-year-olds got screamed at for acting like five-year-olds.

INTERVIEWER: Too bad.

BUCKET BRIGADE: That's life.

(The BUCKET BRIGADE pours the bucket into the pool. The pool glistens. The BUCKET BRIGADE exits.)

INTERVIEWER: So where were we? Oh yes, you were blabbing like a nutcase. From what I've read in your file, I think there's an excellent chance you'll be admitted here.

APPLICANT: Whew.

INTERVIEWER: However, we want to know you'll fit in.

APPLICANT: Well, I don't know how to play golf, but I'm a great bowler.

INTERVIEWER: In deeper ways. You know how before an insurance plan will accept you, you have to get a total physical?

APPLICANT: Uh-huh.

INTERVIEWER: Well, before you can be accepted into heaven, you have to get a total spiritual.

APPLICANT: A what?

INTERVIEWER: We want to make sure you don't pollute the atmosphere here with immature or corrupted karma.

APPLICANT: You're concerned about karma here?

INTERVIEWER: Definitely.

APPLICANT: Is this a Judeo-Christian heaven, or did I end up in the Buddhist wing?

INTERVIEWER: I'm so sick of that question. Look, it's like this: you take a pie, and you divide it into sections. Each section is a different religion. But it's all one pie. (*Becoming furious for a moment:*) *And you idiots down there keep having wars over whose piece of pie is best!!!!* (*Calms down.*) Sorry. I died in the Crusades. I'm still working it through. So, are you ready for your spiritual?

APPLICANT: I guess so.

INTERVIEWER: Let's start with a simple spiritual history.

APPLICANT: Okay.

INTERVIEWER: Do you have any history of: impatience, jealousy, greed, hostility, hypocrisy, cruelty, grandiosity, immaturity, maliciousness, deceit, pettiness, petulance, prejudice, puerility, procrastination, pugnaciousness, pomposity, paranoia, or sloth?

APPLICANT: Yes.

INTERVIEWER: Which ones?

APPLICANT: All of them . . . on occasion.

INTERVIEWER: I see. (*Writes on a form:*) "Honest and self-aware."
Excellent. Have you ever—uh-oh.

APPLICANT: What?

INTERVIEWER: I didn't see this page when I was—*Holy*— . . . Look at
all these sins. Whoa. You're going to hell.

APPLICANT: What?!

INTERVIEWER: Yep, you're going to hell.

APPLICANT: No! No! *No!!!!!!!!!!*

INTERVIEWER: (*Looks at the APPLICANT, then:*) Just kidding.
(*Writes:*) "Handles shock reasonably well." . . . Of course, given your
sins, if you *are* accepted here, you won't be able to enjoy its pleasures
until you work off all your misdeeds.

APPLICANT: How long will that take?

INTERVIEWER: (*Using calculator:*) Let's see . . . not calling your
mother often enough, refusing to recycle aluminum, saying "I love you"
just because you felt horny, saying "I love you" just because you felt
guilty, saying "I love you" just because you felt sleepy . . . and then we
got the deadlies . . . the venals . . . the misdemeanors . . . 43,324 years.

APPLICANT: 43,324 years?!

INTERVIEWER: Only 10,831 of them are leap years.

APPLICANT: Um, I think you made a mistake.

INTERVIEWER: Never have, never will.

APPLICANT: I know I was no saint, but I wasn't *that* bad.

INTERVIEWER: That's not your decision.

APPLICANT: This isn't fair.

INTERVIEWER: That's not your decision, either.

APPLICANT: It's not fair, damn it! *It's not fair!!!*

INTERVIEWER: (*Writes:*) "Capacity for anger, excellent."

(*A member of the BUCKET BRIGADE enters.*)

BUCKET BRIGADE: Excuse me.

INTERVIEWER: Busy day, huh?

BUCKET BRIGADE: Oh, yeah. A lot of people getting laid off, and a lot of divorces, and also some marriage proposals and babies getting born.

(*The BUCKET BRIGADE pours the bucket into the pool. The pool glistens.*)

INTERVIEWER: Well, I'm glad there's some balance.

(*The BUCKET BRIGADE exits.*)

Well, let's see. Between the test questions and our initial conversation, you tested very high on basic emotional range and strength, and I see by your file that, despite some forgivable flaws, you have a great deal of compassion, open-mindedness, lovingkindness, and humility. (*Reviews notes, and then:*) Welcome to Heaven.

APPLICANT: You mean it?

INTERVIEWER: I think you'll enjoy it here—for a long time.

APPLICANT: Wow. By the way, I have a couple of close dead friends. Are they—

INTERVIEWER: Oh, yes, um, sorry. They didn't make it.

APPLICANT: Are you sure?

INTERVIEWER: Positive.

APPLICANT: But they were so—

INTERVIEWER: We know things you don't.

APPLICANT: How about my parents?

INTERVIEWER: Nope.

APPLICANT: My grandmother?

INTERVIEWER: Burning.

APPLICANT: But she was the sweetest—

INTERVIEWER: Fried grandma.

APPLICANT: But, but, but . . .

INTERVIEWER: I know. Would you like a tissue?

APPLICANT: No, thanks.

INTERVIEWER: You can cry. I won't judge.

APPLICANT: I, I . . . I don't cry.

INTERVIEWER: Never?

APPLICANT: Not since I was a little kid.

INTERVIEWER: Not when your friends died, or your parents, or your gr—

APPLICANT: No.

INTERVIEWER: I see. (*Writes, and then looks up:*) All those people you mentioned, they're here.

APPLICANT: Oh, whew. That's such a—

INTERVIEWER: But you can't come in yet. Sorry.

APPLICANT: Ohhh . . . Oh, oh, oh. This is another test, isn't it?

INTERVIEWER: No, the test is over. I promise.

APPLICANT: You're kidding.

INTERVIEWER: Do you want me to swear on a Bible? We've got lots of 'em.

APPLICANT: I'm, I'm going to hell?

INTERVIEWER: No. I said you can't come in *yet*.

APPLICANT: How long bef—

INTERVIEWER: I'm afraid you have an impaired capacity for grieving. The ramifications of that are very—well, people who can't grieve, they're dangerous.

APPLICANT: I wouldn't hurt a—

INTERVIEWER: Not to bodies. To souls. Don't worry. You're not the first person with this problem. That's why we have . . . this pool of tears.

(The BUCKET BRIGADE enters during this conversation.)

APPLICANT: Pool of tears?

(The BUCKET BRIGADE pours the bucket into the pool. The pool glistens.)

INTERVIEWER: When tears evaporate, they rise *above* the clouds, and we collect them here. If you soak in the pool long enough, it will soften your resistance, and it'll reconnect you to a place where tears are a source of comfort instead of shame.

(The BUCKET BRIGADE exits. The INTERVIEWER leads the APPLICANT to the pool.)

APPLICANT: I, uh, I can't get in there.

INTERVIEWER: Sure you can. I'll help.

APPLICANT: No. I really can't get in there.

INTERVIEWER: Let me help.

APPLICANT: Let go!

INTERVIEWER: Calm down.

APPLICANT: I don't know how to swim!

INTERVIEWER: So?

APPLICANT: So I could drown!

INTERVIEWER: So?

APPLICANT: Then I'll— . . . Moot point, huh?

INTERVIEWER: You'd be amazed how many people in heaven take up skydiving. . . . If you go in slowly, you'll be fine.

(The INTERVIEWER helps the APPLICANT into the pool. The APPLICANT holds on to the side of the pool. The APPLICANT's legs rise to the surface.)

APPLICANT: This isn't bad . . . Hey, look. My legs are up. I'm—I'm floating.

INTERVIEWER: Of course you are. Tears are made of salt water. They buoy you up.

(The APPLICANT relaxes in the water.)

END OF PLAY

TURK, TURK, TURK

Deirdre Girard

Deirdre Girard, who tells women's stories, received her playwriting MFA at Boston University. She has had dozens of award-winning short plays produced both nationally and internationally, as well as two full-length plays. Several of her short plays have been published in anthologies or with script services. Deirdre was named a Playwriting Fellow at New Repertory Theatre two years in a row and was selected for both the Company One PlayLab and Central Square Theater's TWSS play development program. She is a playwriting instructor/mentor for several organizations, including Gloucester Stage, the Massachusetts Young Playwrights' Project, and Northeastern University's Silver Masque Theatre Company. Additionally, Deirdre is a member of the advisory council for Boston Playwrights' Theatre and Boston University's MFA playwriting program and is an editor for StageSource's New England New Play Alliance Newsletter. Learn more on her New Play Exchange profile (newplayexchange.org).

SYNOPSIS

When bombastic Danny barges over to his new neighbor Michael's house to confront him about his son feeding the turkeys, he finds out there are much bigger issues at play than a little turkey crap on his patio . . .

CHARACTERS

DANNY, 50–60, a rough and tumble working-class guy.
MICHAEL, 30–40, more sophisticated than Danny, with a touch of sarcasm under the surface.

SETTING

The backyard of Michael's suburban home.

TIME

The present.

MICHAEL is in his yard doing yardwork. His neighbor DANNY approaches.

DANNY: How you doing there?

MICHAEL: Great! Beautiful day.

DANNY: I'm Danny from next door.

MICHAEL: (*Extending his hand.*) Michael.

DANNY: I know we should've been over here with donuts or whatnot before now . . .

MICHAEL: No worries, I'm happy to meet you.

DANNY: Maybe a bar-b-cue this summer. You know, to welcome you and the family.

MICHAEL: It's just me and my son. But thanks, that would be great.

DANNY: That's what the wife thought, because she didn't see any woman around.

MICHAEL: No, not anymore.

DANNY: But the kid's with you?

MICHAEL: Bobby. Yeah. Most of the time anyway.

DANNY: Huh.

> (*An awkward moment while DANNY kind of shuffles his feet and looks off, avoiding what he came to say.*)

MICHAEL: Can I get you a beer or something?

DANNY: No, no. I just thought I'd maybe talk to you about the turkey situation.

MICHAEL: I can't believe how many we have in the yard. Bobby's crazy about them.

DANNY: Yeah. About that . . .

MICHAEL: (*Excited.*) Did you see all the babies this morning? I was drinking my coffee, I look out, and there had to be six, maybe seven of those fuzzy little chicks following their—

DANNY: Frickin' turkeys. Breed like rats.

MICHAEL: Oh.

DANNY: And crap all over the patio. Have you seen their crap?

MICHAEL: Um, no, I don't think so . . .

DANNY: Bigger than my dog's. The wife's having fits cleaning it up all the time. Plus, they get aggressive like you don't know.

MICHAEL: These guys seem pretty tame . . .

DANNY: They're not. Give them an inch, next thing you know they'll be pecking at their own reflection in your car door. Wife has fits about that too.

MICHAEL: Well, I'll keep an eye out. Thanks for stopping over.

DANNY: Birdbrain. Shows you where they got that expression.

MICHAEL: (*With a hint of sarcasm that goes over DANNY's head.*) You're right. Pretty fitting.

DANNY: I'm thinking I might just thin out the herd one of these days . . .

MICHAEL: Um . . . I'm not sure that would be—

DANNY: Don't worry, I'd do it at night. I don't need those animal rights types all over my ass.

MICHAEL: You probably don't want to fire a gun with neighbors so close . . .

DANNY: Nah, I wouldn't do that.

MICHAEL: Oh, okay, good, for a minute there—

DANNY: I was thinking poison.

MICHAEL: Whoa . . .

DANNY: We have to do something! This is my goddamned yard, not theirs.

MICHAEL: Actually, this is my yard.

DANNY: You know the only way to stop a pest?

MICHAEL: We're talking about the turkeys?

DANNY: Don't make them feel welcome.

(*DANNY suddenly runs toward the audience, shouting, wildly waving his hands and stomping his feet.*)

SHOO, SHOO, YOU MOTHERFUCKERS! (*Watching the "turkeys" scatter, then turning back to MICHAEL in triumph.*) You see that?

MICHAEL: Okay, thanks, I'll keep it in mind. (*Moving toward his house in the hope of ending the conversation.*) So anyway, nice to meet you . . .

DANNY: Biggest no-no with these birds?

MICHAEL: (*Reluctantly turning back.*) Um . . . no idea.

DANNY: Feeding them.

MICHAEL: Oh.

DANNY: I seen your boy out feeding them, and if he keeps it up, they'll keep coming. Keep breeding. Keep crapping all over the place.

(*A few moments of silence as DANNY waits for a response that doesn't come.*)

I hate to be a jerk coming over here with a complaint, you being new and all.

MICHAEL: Well, we're out of bread, so Bobby won't be feeding them today.

DANNY: Not just today—he can't feed them at all. Not ever.

MICHAEL: Hang on there . . . not that it's any of your business, but Bobby kind of gets stuck on things, he really doesn't take change well.

DANNY: Who the hell does?

MICHAEL: And the only thing that's made him happy since the move out here is the wild turkeys. He feels like the new house came with pets.

DANNY: Yeah, we noticed he was a little off.

MICHAEL: He's not "off." He's on the autism spectrum.

DANNY: Right. We suspected something like that. Sorry.

MICHAEL: Don't be. He's a great kid.

DANNY: No doubt that. None at all. Me and the wife would love to meet him. But he has to stop feeding the turkeys. Honest to God, if I have to hear the wife nag about cleaning up after them one more time . . .

MICHAEL: Listen, I had no idea it was such a big problem for you—

DANNY: So now you know. (*Leaving.*) And I'm sorry for barging in over here, but I'm glad we cleared this up.

    (DANNY walks several steps away before MICHAEL calls out to him.)

MICHAEL: I . . . hang on . . . just to be clear . . . I'm not going to say anything to Bobby about this.

DANNY: Sorry?

MICHAEL: Not right now anyway.

DANNY: Could you maybe just get him a hamster or something else to feed?

MICHAEL: I wish it were that simple.

DANNY: You're the parent, you don't want to be giving him the upper hand . . .

MICHAEL: He won't understand.

DANNY: Ah. You're one of these "explaining things" kind of parents. Just tell him what I told you. About the crap and all.

MICHAEL: Tell him? No. I can't tell him things.

DANNY: You just gotta—

MICHAEL: No! There's nothing I can do, there's nothing I haven't tried! Trust me! I mean, apparently, the biggest problem in your life right now is turkey shit. But I can't even get Bobby to understand basic things, like the fact that we had to move to be near a specialized school—he's just pissed off at me for changing his routine. He doesn't know what it's like to have a friend or join the Boy Scouts or play ball with the other kids. He has no idea why his mother left us, and I'm not even sure he actually realizes she left. And when I tell him I love him . . . I don't know if that means anything to him at all. I hope it does, but I just don't know.

DANNY: Oh man, that sucks.

MICHAEL: Yeah it does. For that poor little guy.

DANNY: And for you.

MICHAEL: Not compared to what his world must be like.

DANNY: Is it gonna get better?

MICHAEL: Maybe with this new school. That's the hope.

DANNY: I feel like a real asshole now.

MICHAEL: Don't. I shouldn't have said all that . . . I'm just overwhelmed and short-tempered with . . . whatever . . . with this move and everything.

DANNY: The move? You got a lot more than that going on here. And the wife leaving you too.

MICHAEL: Yeah. Apparently, this wasn't her dream.

DANNY: Ain't nobody's. But being a parent's not about us and what we want, am I right?

MICHAEL: You bet.

DANNY: He's a sweet kid. I can tell that.

MICHAEL: He really is.

DANNY: Me and the wife, we love kids. And you know what? Your kid's more important than turkey shit.

MICHAEL: (*Laughing.*) Thanks.

DANNY: No, I mean it. To tell the truth, it's actually kind of peaceful watching him out here with the turkeys. It's like they calm down a little when he's around, they're less savage, like they know he needs them.

MICHAEL: He definitely connects with animals . . .

DANNY: And listening to him. Turk, Turk, Turk. Like a song almost. Calling in those turkeys. Kind of cute. Turk, Turk, Turk. Even makes the wife smile. And man she hates those flying rats.

MICHAEL: He's not actually talking . . .

DANNY: Sure he is. Turk, Turk, Turk.

MICHAEL: It's just guttural sounds.

DANNY: You're saying you haven't heard him?

MICHAEL: He likes to be on his own when he feeds them, but—

DANNY: The wife says he's the turkey whisperer. Whatever that means.

MICHAEL: That would be wonderful. But I'm telling you, Bobby doesn't speak at all.

DANNY: Maybe not to you. But he definitely talks to them damn turkeys.

(*Several beats.*)

MICHAEL: Are you sure?

DANNY: Turk, Turk, Turk. Clear as a bell.

MICHAEL: And it's not just—

DANNY: It's real words!

MICHAEL: It's hard to . . . I mean, I knew it was possible . . .

(*MICHAEL is a bit overcome, close to tears. DANNY does not know where to look and is growing uncomfortable, starting to shuffle his feet awkwardly again.*)

DANNY: I didn't mean to go making you all emotional or whatever . . .

MICHAEL: Sorry, I . . . you have no idea what this means . . . you're positive?

DANNY: (*Holding up his hand like he's swearing on a Bible.*) Hand to God! (*Taking out his cell phone and dialing.*) Hang on. I'm gonna prove it to you. (*On phone.*) Listen, honey. I need you to do something right now . . . I don't care about your show, just pay attention here, this is important. Grab up every piece of bread in the house and come over next door—I mean everything—every roll, those frozen waffle things, the Pop Tarts . . . Just get your butt over here with the bread and I'll explain.

(*Hangs up, then to MICHAEL:*)

Go get your boy. We've got some turkeys to feed.

(*Lights down.*)

END OF PLAY

WISHES

Mark Harvey Levine

Mark Harvey Levine has had more than 1,800 productions of his plays everywhere from Bangalore to Bucharest and from Lima to London. His plays have won more than forty-five awards and have been produced in more than ten languages. Full evenings of his plays, such as *Cabfare for the Common Man*, *Didn't See That Coming*, and *A Very Special Holiday Special* have been shown around the world, including a multiyear tour of Brazil. A Spanish-language film of *The Kiss* (*El Beso*) premiered at Cannes and aired on HBO and dTV (Japan). His plays appear in other Applause anthologies, such as *10-Minute Plays for Kids*, *Men's Comedic Monologues That Are Actually Funny*, and *Duo! The Best Scenes for Two for the 21st Century*. Website: markharveylevine.com.

SYNOPSIS

Scott has the unique ability to pick up coins in a fountain and read people's wishes. But it's ruining his life.

CHARACTERS

REBECCA, 30s, pragmatic, currently very upset.
SCOTT, 30s, a dreamer.

SETTING

A city fountain.

TIME

Late afternoon.

NOTE

The fountain can be just an area set off on the stage.

A city fountain. SCOTT is standing in the fountain wearing hip waders (or with his pants rolled up), scooping up the coins that people have thrown into the water and looking at them. REBECCA angrily approaches him.

REBECCA: I knew it. I knew I'd find you here.

SCOTT: I had a free half hour! I just—

REBECCA: This is an addiction, Scott. It's an addiction.

SCOTT: I just like it, okay? It relaxes me. It's fun.

REBECCA: It's taken over your life.

SCOTT: I find it fascinating. All these wishes—

(He holds up a coin.)

This lady wishes she could see São Paulo again before she dies. São Paulo!

REBECCA: I don't care! It's become an obsession with you.

SCOTT: It's really not. It's just something I enjoy. Like fishing. Or . . . or stamp collecting. I collect wishes. Who am I hurting?

REBECCA: Me, Scott. You're hurting me. This is time away from me. From us.

SCOTT: Just a half hour! If I went to a bar, nobody would blink an eye. But stand in a fountain, and suddenly I'm . . . an addict? I've got a problem?

REBECCA: Yes, you've got a problem.

SCOTT: Come in with me, Rebecca. It's fun. You used to like to do this with me. I've got your hip waders in the car . . .

REBECCA: I did it because *you* liked it, Scott. Not because I did. I did it for you. Okay? Now I'm asking you to do something for me. I'm asking you to stop. It's ruining our relationship.

SCOTT: Oh my God, now I'm ruining our relationship? Because I'm looking at some coins?

REBECCA: You're ruining our relationship because you'd rather stand in a fountain than be at home with me.

SCOTT: Look, it's just a few wishes . . . it's interesting . . . this person wants their dog to come back—

REBECCA: You want some wishes, Scott? I'll give you some wishes.

(*She digs into her pocket and comes up with a handful of coins. She throws a coin at SCOTT; he flinches.*)

I wish you didn't have this stupid ability or whatever it is! (*Throws another coin at him.*) I wish you wanted to be with me instead of all these strangers! (*Throws another coin at him.*) I wish I was more important to you than them! (*Throws another coin at him.*) I wish *we* were more important to you! I wish—

(*She throws another coin at him, and he catches it.*)

SCOTT: Don't.

REBECCA: I wish I'd never met you!

(SCOTT stands there for a moment, holding the coin, looking at her sadly.)

SCOTT: Your wish has been granted.

(REBECCA stares at him, blinking. Then she looks at him curiously. She's never met him before.)

(Softly.) Goodbye.

(He goes back to looking at coins. She starts to leave but comes back.)

REBECCA: Hey!

SCOTT: *(Surprised.)* Hey.

REBECCA: Whatcha doin'?

SCOTT: Um, you won't believe me.

REBECCA: Sure I will.

SCOTT: No, trust me, you won't. Not at first anyway.

REBECCA: Are you stealing those coins?

SCOTT: No! No. I'm . . . collecting wishes.

REBECCA: You're what, now?

SCOTT: I have this . . . ability. Or talent. You know how people throw coins into a fountain and make a wish? I can pick up the coin and tell you what the wish was.

REBECCA: Get outta town.

SCOTT: I'm serious. *(Going through some coins.)* Look . . . this guy wants to date the cute analyst at his job. This lady would like to live in a nicer house. A lot of them wish for money. Which is ironic, considering they're actually throwing money away. But still . . .

REBECCA: You're making this up.

SCOTT: I swear it's true. It's incredibly fascinating. You can tell a lot about people by what they wish for. And sometimes . . . if it's a really heartfelt wish . . . I can even make their wishes come true.

REBECCA: (*Laughs.*) So you're a genie?

SCOTT: Nah, I'm just a regular guy. With one peculiar little talent.

REBECCA: (*Smiling.*) I think you're crazy.

SCOTT: Still don't believe me? Come on. Make a wish. I'll tell you what it is. It looks like you were about to, anyway.

(*She looks down; she's still holding some coins in her hand.*)

REBECCA: Huh . . . I guess I was. Okay, tell me what I'm wishing for.

(*She lightly tosses a coin to him, and he catches it.*)

SCOTT: Hmmm . . . you have wished for . . . (*Laughs.*) A hot fudge sundae?

REBECCA: (*He's right.*) Oh my God.

SCOTT: With chopped peanuts.

REBECCA: How did you do that?! What is it, some kind of magic trick?

SCOTT: I told you. It's my special little skill.

REBECCA: That's amazing. That's absolutely amazing!

SCOTT: Wild, isn't it? These coins are all the wishes of people who have been here before us. And I can read every single one.

REBECCA: If I could do what you do, I would never leave this fountain!

SCOTT: I know! It *is* kind of addicting. Actually, I'm thinking of giving it up.

REBECCA: You're kidding. Why?

(He starts to come out of the fountain.)

SCOTT: I found something better. I'm Scott, by the way.

REBECCA: Rebecca.

(They shake hands.)

SCOTT: It's going to be different this time.

REBECCA: What?

SCOTT: Nothing. Hey, can I buy you that hot fudge sundae?

REBECCA: Oh you really don't have to, it was just the first thing that came to my—

SCOTT: I know but . . . I told you I can make some wishes come true. I think I can definitely handle this one. There's this great little place right down the block. I know you're really going to like it. Besides, when was the last time you had dessert with a guy in hip waders? (*Or if you don't have hip waders: ". . . a guy with wet feet?"*)

REBECCA: (*Laughs.*) Y'know, I can't even remember . . .

(They start to leave, then—)

SCOTT: Hang on.

(He takes a coin out of his pocket. Holds it, makes a silent wish, and throws it into the fountain. Then they exit.)

END OF PLAY